LITERARY STRUCTURES
Edited by John Gardner

The
Construction
of the
Wakefield Cycle

by JOHN GARDNER

SOUTHERN ILLINOIS UNIVERSITY PRESS
Carbondale and Edwardsville

Feffer & Simons, Inc.
London and Amsterdam

Library of Congress Cataloging in Publication Data

Gardner, John, 1933–
   The construction of the Wakefield cycle.

   (Literary structures)
   Includes bibliographical references.
   1. English drama—To 1500—History and criticism.
2. Pageants—Wakefield, England. 3. Towneley plays.
4. Mysteries and miracle—Plays, English—History and
criticism. I. Title II. Title: Wakefield cycle.
PR644.W3G3   822'.051   74-5191
ISBN 0-8093-0665-4

For my mother

Contents

Acknowledgments

For the texts of the Towneley MS pageants I have used *The Towneley Plays,* ed. George England and A. W. Pollard, EETS, ES 71 (London, 1897), except in the case of the plays edited by A. C. Cawley in *The Wakefield Pageants in the Towneley Cycle* (Manchester, 1958), a book which includes only the pageants regularly attributed to the Wakefield Master. Quotations from the Cawley edition are reprinted by permission of Manchester University Press. (I had hoped to use the new Cawley and Stevens edition of the complete cycle but at this writing it has still not seen print.) Texts of other plays used here are normally *The Chester Plays,* ed. Hermann Deimling and Dr. Matthews, Parts 1 and 2 EETS, ES 62 and 115 (London, 1892 and 1896); *The Digby Plays,* ed. F. J. Furnivall, EETS, ES 70 (London, 1922); *York Plays,* ed. Lucy Toulmin Smith (1885; reprinted, New York, 1963); and *The Non-Cycle Mystery Plays,* ed. O. Waterhouse, EETS, ES 104 (London, 1909).

I thank the editors of the *Educational Theatre Journal* and *Papers on Language and Literature* for permission to reprint here, in revised form, various essays which originally appeared in those journals. Chapter 2, here revised, is reprinted by permission of the Modern Language Association of America from "Theme and Irony in the Wakefield *Mactacio Abel,*" *PMLA* 80 (1965), 515–21. Copyright 1965 by the Modern Language Association of America.

The Construction of the Wakefield Cycle

PROLOGUE

The Wakefield Pageants

At the time I began writing this book, ten years ago, most medieval-ists scoffed at the idea of subjecting mystery plays to close literary analysis. Now close analysis is so much the standard approach to the plays, shrewd readers may scoff at my frittering away a whole book on such business. My excuses are as follows. First, what this book tries to give is an overview of the Wakefield *Corpus Christi* play as a unified—though hardly perspicuous—work of art. I look closely at each of the more important pageants, showing fundamental rela-tionships between them, and glance more hastily at shorter, cruder pageants, indicating how they work within the total scheme. Having set up this overview, I go on to offer a theory of how the enormous play was made. Second, I write with a different purpose from that of most medievalists who comment on the plays. I write not primar-ily for specialists in search of out-of-the-way information but for student-medievalists and literary generalists, people whose chief con-cern is aesthetic. Ideally, of course, I should publish a decent trans-lation (or modernization) of the pageants—but if I did, it would need an introduction as long and tedious as this book, because the pageants, as specialists know, are tricky. I have, in fact, done some work on a translation; that was one of the projects that distracted me from this study. But translation of a work like the Wakefield *Corpus Christi* play is tortuous and slow, particularly since there is no good text to work from. Sooner or later the difficulty of it all drives you back, for a while at least, to criticism.

It seems to me that even now, in some respects, critics have not adequately understood the method of the mystery pageants, even the comic Wakefield pageants so frequently praised as exceptional.[1] I point out in this book reasons for believing we may have been over-confident in assigning certain of the Towneley MS pageants to the Wakefield Master and dismissing others as the work of lesser men.

If we concentrate principally on the more obvious features of the technique found in the Wakefield pageants—the characteristic stanza, the randy language, the social criticism—we find the pageants un-usual. But if we look at other, less obvious features of the technique found here, such as the thematic use of verbal repetition, the ironic use of scriptural typology, the consistent manipulation of patterns of imagery (especially satanic imagery), and the oddly modern cutting of transitional devices, we find distinct similarities between such su-perficially dissimilar works as the *Mactacio Abel* and the *Abraham,* or the *Magnus Herodes* and the *Conspiracio.* We find some, though not all, of these same devices in other cycles—Chester, Hegge (or "N. Town"), and York—but seldom are the devices worked out with the same degree of skill. And only here in the Towneley MS do we find that a few basic ideas organize the entire drama from Crea-tion to Judgment.

And so it seems to me likely that the Wakefield Master may have played a far larger part in the composition of the Wakefield cycle than has generally been supposed. Even in pageants which show his characteristic stanza, language, and humor, we find—as in the cycle as a whole—crude work alongside polished, early examples of pag-eant construction alongside late, and narrowly doctrinal material alongside imaginative elaborations of doctrinal points. What I sug-gest is that this single poet may have revised and reshaped the entire cycle in much the way we know he revised and reshaped an early Cain play, parts of which survive in *Mactacio Abel.*

None of this is to deny the standard opinion that the hodgepodge of forms and styles in the cycle as a whole, as well as in pageants assigned to one reviser, shows mystery cycle evolution to be, *in gen-eral,* a process of gradual accretion wherein, in a given town, new or longer pageants were created whenever new guilds joined the fes-tival of *Corpus Christi* and needed something to stage.[2] My theory simply argues that at a late stage of cycle evolution, one poet took the whole hodgepodge in hand and, by ingenious revision and some rewriting, shaped the collection into an artistic unity. Neither does my theory rule out the account brought down by the Towneley family,[3] that the pageants were written or adapted by members of a cell of Augustinian or Black Canons at Widkirk (Woodkirk) near Wakefield. I argue only that however many poets helped to write the cycle, they worked according to one writer's plan.

Even when written or adapted by well-educated churchmen,[4] mystery pageants were a folk art. Pageants developed or borrowed from somewhere else for the York cycle were modified and produced at nearby Wakefield very much as traditional ballads have been transported from place to place and sometimes significantly and artfully modified. To prove that a play "works" is not the same as proving it the creation of some individual genius. Both the famous Child version of "Little Musgrave and Lady Barnard" and John Jacob Niles's version of "Matty Groves"[5] are coherent, though they do not use the same details or have, even, the same theme. The change of a few lines can make all the difference. Professor Vinaver has made clear the absurdity of arguing that a "well made" medieval work must be the product of individual composition and that a work which contains inconsistencies or self-contradiction must be assigned to traditional composition.[6] By this standard, Faulkner's novels are all by several hands, and "Matty Groves" is an original poem composed by John Jacob Niles. What counts, then, is not that the Wakefield pageants are "well made" but that they are made by a limited set of aesthetic rules—rules not operative in other pageant cycles.

Sometimes the Wakefield-pageant reviser or revisers were satisfied with relatively minor changes, recasting and reinterpreting older material, perhaps borrowing heavily from cycles now lost; at other times these writers built from the ground up, as in the *Secunda Pastorum*. Pageants which preserve large chunks of some older work offer evidence that the reviser or revisers sometimes thought it sufficient merely to make dull texts more interesting; and often what the reviser did in such cases was not only to add the comic realism so obvious to modern readers, but also, and equally important, to increase the intellectual subtlety of the pageants and, at the same time, to increase dramatic intensity by cutting slow transitions in the action, breaking up dialogue, elaborating characterization, and introducing suspense and dramatic irony. Certain pageants which contain no trace of humor, such as the *Abraham* and the *Resurreccio Domini,* have this same intellectual subtlety, dramatic intensity, and irony.

The appearance of these characteristics pretty much throughout the Towneley manuscript suggests not only the work of some controlling intelligence but also that in the Wakefield cycle we are dealing with drama which has moved farther beyond the original conventions of the English mystery than has drama from, say, Chester or Hegge. It becomes worthwhile to ask again just what the mystery pageant was in its earlier, simpler form—or, more bluntly, why a thing so dull to us was so appealing to the people of its day, uneducated people, generally speaking, but presumably people not completely wanting in sense. It is useful to ask, too, what relationship, if any, the techniques found in the fully evolved pageants have to techniques in later drama.

Before we turn to these questions, it may be well to comment on certain once common objections to studying the "art" of the mystery pageants at all. Needless to say, the only solid proof that a pageant is worth analysis is the analysis itself: a literary critic makes his case not by arguing that the case can be made but by making it. Moreover, the important scholarly work which has been done on relationships between the mystery pageants and Christian typology,[7] between the pageants and medieval church art,[8] and so forth, may make any apology for close reading of the pageants seem unnecessary. But at least for some readers, objections to close reading of the pageants may need to be reviewed, not only because the objections have sometimes come from important scholars but also because they involve assumptions which may need to be reconsidered.

It is true, within limits, that in the mystery pageants we are dealing with what Hardin Craig has described as "a communal, anonymous, traditional drama the choice of whose subjects was predetermined . . . and whose end and aim was not dramatic but religious."[9] (The limits, as Professor Hardison has shown, are in the implications of the contrastive words *dramatic* and *religious*.) The skeptic may feel, as does Professor Craig, that since the pageants were written or adapted anonymously for a mainly devotional purpose, and since the audience for whom they were performed was not Chaucer's aristocratic audience but the uneducated common man, close study of the pageants must be pointless.

On the communal and anonymous composition of the pageants hardly any comment should be necessary. *Beowulf* is anonymous; Shakespeare's *Hamlet* is partly a selection of old materials. As for what truly communal work could achieve in the Middle Ages, think of Chartres cathedral, or of that vastly elaborated literary leviathan of the twelfth and thirteenth centuries, the so-called Vulgate Cycle of Arthurian romances.

The argument that the mystery pageants are devotional and therefore not dramatic—not concerned with any "deliberate search for dramatic effects"—is almost as easily dismissed. Various critics have expressed their dissatisfaction with the older point of view by attempting to deny that the pageants are religious in the first place.[10] John Spiers, most vocal of these dissenters, argues that the plays are rooted in pre-Christian ritual—a theory no one but Spiers any longer accepts.[11] Professor Hardison, who grants the thorough Christianity of the plays, takes a more devastating line, a line I believe all sober judgment must accept. He calls attention again to the existence of an early and independent vernacular tradition—"consciously composed works, written for a theater that already possessed definite traditions of staging and acting, and conceived from the beginning as representation"—and he shows that the once common scholarly practice of tracing all the vernacular plays back to liturgy and to Latin tropes of the *Quem Quaeritis* type is not in accord with the evidence; that, in fact, there is no reason to believe that certain of the plays (e.g., *Adam* and *Cain*) were ever produced, in any form, inside a church.[12] Hardison is surely right: the vernacular plays did not originate solely within the church. At the same time Hardison makes it impossible for serious scholars to deny that, whatever their origin, the mystery plays, both early and late, simple and complex, are emphatically, in Miss Prosser's words, "a community drama of worship and celebration."[13] The pageants did not stop serving religion as they gained in popularity, though secondary motives for producing them must have gained in importance. In the mid-sixteenth century William Newhall says of one of the most doctrinal and undramatic cycles that these pageants were not only for "increase of the holy and catholic faith of our Savyour, Jhu' Crist, and to exort the mynds of the co'mon people to good devotion and holsome doctryne thereof, but also for the co'mon Welth and prosperitie of this Citie. . . ."[14] If the solemn Chester cycle had economic value, we may be sure that the more "realistic" pageants of the great fifteenth-century trading centers York and Wakefield did too. The pageants were mounted by guilds, whose orientation was presumably more economic than pious. Religious orders did little more than the writing or revising.

Professor Craig explains the evolution of the pageants as follows: "New plays came into existence in response to the growth, very rapid in places like York, in the number of trading companies that wished to have a part in the great annual festival. Such new plays were usually the result of the expansion into a separate play of what had been a mere episode in some other play."[15] The canon of events appropriate to the *Corpus Christi* redemption theme was more or less fixed.[16] The obvious means of expanding scriptural subjects, that is, changing mere episodes into separate pageants, was to dilate scenes by the introduction of more fully developed characters and situations drawn from contemporary life—the activities of shepherds, the legalistic prattle of stupid judges. Both at York and at Wakefield, and frequently elsewhere, these forms of improvisation are evident.

As realistic modern scenes expanded, actual social and psychological problems of medieval men naturally drew the playwrights' increasing attention, particularly if the playwright was a close observer of life; but such concerns cannot be set down at once as secular—they are by no means uncommon in medieval sermons, homiletic poems, and the like. Humor for its own sake was at times introduced, whether by the performer who found he had a talent for making people laugh or by the writer who wished to capitalize on the natural popularity of funny scenes. Perhaps it is true, as Miss Prosser thinks, that this tended now and then to subvert the original motive of the pageants.[17] But against the tendency to introduce humor for its own sake there were important checks. The church, or at all events certain churchmen, disapproved of such debasing of the pageants; the tradition of the pageants was devotional, in fact largely parallel in form to the Mass as allegorized by Amalarius and others;[18] and even at their most realistic the pageants remained, at least in theory, a religious exercise. Considering these checks, it is not surprising to find that as a rule humorous elaboration of scriptural subjects introduces not only comic relief but also serious exploration, from a religious point of view, of contemporary problems. Sometimes this exploration is both literal and allegorical, employing the more obvious emblems used in popular sermons of the day.

The fact that a pageant is religious does not in fact rule out artistic consciousness. Whereas straight dramatization of God's plan for man's redemption was a doctrinal and public matter, social criticism and commentary on the actual behavior of medieval husbands and wives were to a certain extent matters of personal observation. At the same time, even with respect to characterization and the development of conflicts between characters, we must be cautious about calling the playwright's impulse secular. His selection of characters and attitudes to be held up for comic ridicule bears a striking resemblance to the selection made by the medieval preacher, the writer of books on virtues and vices, or the homiletic poet. The medieval preacher does not make much use of humor, admittedly, but humor is a common device in less formal religious writing, especially in poetry. (Miss Prosser's opinion that in late mystery pageants the comedy is occasionally at the expense of religion itself[19] will be dealt with in a later chapter.)

Finally, it is not the case that the devotional impulse rules out any "deliberate search for dramatic effects"—unless we take the word dramatic in an extremely limited sense. Playwrights, like preachers, seek to move and persuade, not simply instruct, and each man moves his audience by the means at his command. In one of the sermons from the British Museum MS. Royal 18 B, xxiii, a collection some of the sermons in which seem to have been composed as preachers' models, we find a short quotation from St. Bernard concerning the Last Judgment, followed by what must be a recommendation to preachers for dramatic—that is, emotionally forceful—expansion of the subject: "And þat þis is dredefull, narrate þe xv signis"—a reference to the well known fifteen signs of approaching Doom.[20] Instances of this sort of thing might be enumerated at length, but no such labor should be necessary for the present point. It was one of the preacher's jobs to make Christian doctrine persuasive, and he did his job by piling up stories, by dramatizing for his congregation the torments of hell and the joys of heaven—in other words, by hunting for "effect." The writers of personal meditations do the same. As for religious poets, think of the conscious dramatic effects in *Pearl, Purity, Patience,* and *Sir Gawain,* or think of the *Debate of Body and Soul.* It may be true that the kinds of effects found in the mystery pageants are not the kinds found in Marlowe or Shakespeare; but to insist that the mysteries contain no dramatic effects unless by accident is to misread the pageants.

The once common assumption that nothing intellectually complex will be found in pageants composed for simple and uneducated medieval people is equally mistaken. True, the English middle class of the fourteenth through sixteenth centuries was, in our terms, uneducated. But these people were not as simple as we have sometimes imagined. Though their congregations could not read, medieval preachers could safely allude to a host of biblical stories; artists could employ typology (Isaac carrying faggots in the shape of a cross),[21] and lyric writers could assume an intelligent and fairly subtle audience.

So the question arises: if the audience was not in fact simpleminded, and if playwrights, like preachers, were capable of certain

kinds of subtlety when they chose to use them, how are we to account for the manifest dullness and simplicity of so many of the
pageants? Why were they so well attended throughout England?[22]
One part of the answer is that when the pageants were originally
performed the texts themselves—all that has come down to us except for a few songs—were the least important element. Professor
Swart has pointed out that the traditional notion of the pageant
stages, drawn from the Chester *Breviarye* (wrongly attributed to
Archdeacon Rogers but in fact written by his son after 1609), must
be replaced by a view of the pageant stages as complex structures
equipped with traps, hoists, and even cloud machines; and he adds
the observation that the English plays give hints that such complex
stages were used there.[23] Like the masques of the time, the plays may
have been quasi-magical spectacles very impressive indeed. (Language
reflects the magical side of medieval theater. The *tragetour* in Old
French was a juggler or montebank; the OED in listings from 1300
to 1340 gives the word the denotation of a man having godlike
or witchlike powers. By 1380 the *tragetour* is grouped with tumblers,
jesters, and japers—he is now an actor, not a priest of the occult.
Yet the actor-entertainers in Chaucer's *House of Fame,* written not
long before 1380, are sorcerers, witches, magicians.) Though actors
in the mystery pageants were not professionals, as a rule, but were
citizens selected by a board of some kind,[24] they were probably in-
fluenced by the professionals of the time; otherwise why the explicit
rules, at York for instance, against the hiring of professionals? In
courtly masques from Chaucer's day to after Ben Jonson's, levita-
tion, ingenious machines of one sort or another, and clever disap-
pearances were a standard part of the entertainment. It is true that
simplified and symbolic props were usual in medieval courtly masques
(as in mystery pageants or, later, the tragedies of Shakespeare), a
single branch signifying a forest, a single soldier signifying an army,
a few chairs signifying an assembly hall; but it is also true that
within the same masque there might appear convincing and elaborately constructed buildings or pavilions, boats, even illusory for-
ests.[25] In other words, stylized representations in courtly medieval
theater were chosen for aesthetic reasons, not because the company
worked with a minimal budget; and the same may have been true
in popular pageants. We see this aesthetic simplification wherever
we look in medieval art—for instance, in the illustrations which
accompany poems, wherein one figure represents a crew of sailors and

two waves represent a storm at sea.[26] We find analogous effects in medieval music.

What was true of the aristocratic masques may also have been true of popular drama—the mystery and morality plays, especially those of the fifteenth century. The guilds which selected actors and provided stage props appropriate to each guild's particular line of work (the "Golde Smythis," for example, outfitted the Magi of the York cycle) must have provided lavishly for the pageants, vying with one another for the spectator's admiration and money. This fits with what we know of the pageant cars created for the Dutch middle class in the sixteenth century.[27] The machinery of a fixed stage, like the stages admired in France, may have been even more spectacular.

If the chief interest of the mystery pageants in their earlier form was visual, then it need not surprise us that, on one hand, the pageants were enormously popular and that, on the other hand, when we look at the texts we discover that, as A. P. Rossiter says, "from the literary point of view the workmanship is never far from crude and, in the older strata, insipid."[28] One might, after all, say the same of the courtly masques. We need not expect "drama" in a masque which requires costumes for fourteen female figures, fourteen bearded men, fourteen angels, fourteen characters with headdresses topped by upside-down legs complete with shoes, fourteen figures with mountainlike heads possibly having rabbits running in and out of tunnels, fourteen dragons, fourteen peacocks, and fourteen swans.[29] Neither is drama inevitable in a Noah pageant put together (as was the one at York) by "Fysshers and Marynars," an Expulsion from Eden pageant put together by "þe Crafte of Armourers," or an Angelic Visitation produced by chandlers. On the other hand, when drama does come into the pageants, we may safely guess that spectacle does not drop out.

With regard to the dullness of the early texts I will simply register here a second point, to be developed at more length later. O. B. Hardison has provided a new principle for judging these texts, that of fidelity to source when the source is biblical or traditionally devotional. It is no accident that in the brilliant Towneley *Extraccio* and *Judicium* pageants the character of Christ remains unchanged, while the roles of devils and villains are richly improvised.

Whereas earlier pageant writers threaded rhymes through engaging spectacles, seeking in their verse only the simplest devotional effects—solemn speeches for Deus, appropriately devout speeches for

Noah and Abraham—more ingenious playwrights emerged in some localities, pressing beyond "theater" to characterization and profluence through conflict. The York Metrist and the Wakefield Master explored the possibility of creating greater immediacy for their dramatized Bible stories by establishing convincing characters, by introducing suspense, and by appealing to men's feeling for poetic style. Such was the evolution of the mystery from spectacle to art. The most important innovation of such poets was their use within the popular drama of an extremely subtle form of the allegorical method which was used, less subtly, in popular sermons of the day, had been used quite openly in earlier mysteries, especially in France and Germany, and was used with the greatest ingenuity by such poets as Dante and Chaucer. Whereas earlier mystery pageants made a point of introducing the traditional exegetical notion that Noah, Isaac, and other Old Testament figures are types or prefigurations of Christ, and explicitly allegorized the literal action for the audience (sometimes, as in the Chester Abraham pageant, by means of an Expositor), later playwrights craftily buried their allegory in the realistic behavior and punning speech of a medievalized Noah or Isaac, and were thus able to express the character's typic identification and at the same time to dramatize every man's involvement in the fundamental mysteries of Christian doctrine. Building on the traditional patristic contrast between the Old Jerusalem—a figure of this world—and the New, they developed a satirical comedy which focused on the pretensions of this world to rivalry with the next. The method of these playwrights is not the one we find characteristic of later drama, which is no doubt why it so long escaped attention; but it is indeed a method—it was still used in Elizabethan times and later—and it was one capable of fine effects. The fully evolved mystery cycle is not a stage in the development of drama as we find it in later ages but a closed evolutionary line, a culmination. Except as such playwrights as Marlowe borrow mystery-play devices (whether by accident or through influence), the individual mystery pageant can no more lead to Renaissance drama than, say, the fully evolved woodcut can lead to painting in oils. The *Corpus Christi* play as a whole is no more closely related to Renaissance drama than the *Iliad* is to the plays of Aeschylus.

In fact, the method of individual mystery pageants at their best is in fundamental conflict with most modern dramatic practice. The basically Aristotelian idea of conflict resulting in a causally related series of events which, taken together, make up a complete action—

Aristotle's *energia* (the actualization of the potential which exists in character and situation)—can have no place in drama based not on a theory of reality as process but on a theory of reality as stasis. If reality is the unchanging Supreme Good, if Nature is God's revelation of Himself in emblematic form, and if the proper response to this mutable world is the search within it for the *vestigia* or traces of God's hand, the immutable principle, then a concern with action is not only unwarranted but perverse, a failure of right reason. Man's whole study should be the implicit unchangeable, the contrast between the physical Israel and the spiritual Israel, Babylon and the City of God. Of course work based on contrast rather than conflict is not really something we need to adjust ourselves to (*pace* D. W. Robertson, Jr., and others).[30] It is the mode of satire from *The Alchemist* to *Pogo*, to speak only of things modern. What satire and Christian drama have in common is an absolute base: as satire depends for its effect on the unquestioned social and ethical values of the audience, Christian drama depends for its effect on unquestionable dogma. In the Wakefield cycle, each individual pageant works in this way; in the Wakefield *Corpus Christi* play as a whole, another, in some ways more modern kind of action, is developed.

I have emphasized the fact that the plays are religious—in subject, in purpose, even in their choice of method. That emphasis is perhaps misleading. I should have said they are "serious," and in medieval England serious thought is, inescapably, religious. To the medieval poet speaking to the middle class, the only terms available for describing human psychology, or for commenting on social problems, or for ridiculing human foibles—are Christian. The real purpose of my commentary on the Towneley MS plays is to demonstrate that if the pageants are religious they are also magnificent theater. Anyone who has looked closely at medieval sermons knows that they are often interesting, often extremely vivid; but the logic of the sermon, however entertaining the sermon may be, is linear—the logic of argument. The logic of the mystery pageants—even the textually dull ones—is poetic: meaning is not merely stated but is released by the juxtaposition of part against part. To speak of the pageants as dramatized sermons is to blur the age-old distinction between discourse and poetry. The distinction is not always clear in the plays themselves, needless to say: art and theology interpenetrate. This is merely to say that sermon content, when transferred to another form, remains itself while becoming something new. Reading the plays as though they were merely primitive plays, not dramas of doctrine, can lead to misapprehension; but studies of, say, the typology in the plays can be equally misleading. Miss Woolf's analysis, several years ago, of the exegetical tradition reflected in the Abraham-Isaac plays[31] revealed the way in which the most casual phrases can call up a rich scriptural association; but her evaluation of the York and Towneley plays was nevertheless wrong, because it ignored important poetic and dramatic effects within the Abraham play and ignored the construction of the Wakefield cycle as a whole. It is true that all Abraham-Isaac plays (or all mystery plays on any other subject) must deal with the same doctrinal matter; but it is not true that all playwrights set out to do exactly the same thing or that they succeed or fail in the same terms. A historical approach to the pageant subjects provides us with the playwright's point of departure, not his play. Some playwrights, of course, never got beyond their point of departure. Others wrote works of art which cannot be appreciated or understood until we have discovered by the techniques of literary criticism the exact reason why everything is as it is and not otherwise.

One last word of prologue. The chapters which follow are not organized as a concentrated development of the theory I wish finally to advance on the construction of the Wakefield cycle. The first few chapters present close readings of individual pageants, laying the groundwork for the overall theory. Later chapters turn increasingly to the problem of placing the individual pageant or pageant group in the context of the *Corpus Christi* play as a whole—the context which explains why they are as they are. The final chapter and the Epilogue deal with the unity of the pageant collection.

ONE

Decorum and Satanic Parody
in the Wakefield *Creation*

All four of the more or less complete English mystery cycles—Chester, Hegge, York, and Wakefield—as well as the earlier Cornish cycle, contain full-blown Creation pageants. It seems clear that the pageants are distantly related: comparison of the texts reveals numerous verbal and structural similarities, some of which I will mention in a moment. No clear direction of influence is discernible. We are apparently dealing not with a sequence of versions but with parallel representatives of a late stage of a very old tradition, one which in fact goes back at least to the twelfth century in Europe. In 1194, in the Lower Bavarian city of Regensburg or Ratisbon, there was a large-scale production "of the Creation of the Angels and the Fall of Lucifer and his followers, of the Creation and Fall of Man, and of the Prophets. . . ."[1] Other plays on the same theme were produced during the thirteenth and fourteenth centuries in Italy and France. Since the Creation is the cornerstone for the whole structure of the *Corpus Christi* drama, we may be sure that every one of the lost English cycles, and all of the Continental cycles as well, had versions of the Creation.

If all the lost pageants could be found it would perhaps be possible to trace the lines along which the Creation pageant evolved (if evolution is relevant here) and to describe without hazard the particular aesthetic virtues of each of the pageants; it might even be possible to isolate some Devonian parent, so to speak, which established the terms of the tradition and gave it its start. But dealing only with the pageants we have, we can see at least this much:

the tradition of the Creation pageant was widespread and relatively stable, so that playwrights building on the tradition had available to them a solid basis for their own adaptation and invention. Pageants from opposite ends of England, probably composed many years apart, have common features impossible to dismiss as coincidental or as inevitable results of the process of dramatizing scripture. For instance, all four English pageants begin with God's declaration that he is alpha and omega, then proceed to elaborate the ideas of beginning and ending appropriate to God's complete plan for man—the subject of the *Corpus Christi* drama as a whole—and, finally, contrast these limits with God's own unlimited nature, never begun and never to be ended. Several of the pageants emphasize God's triune nature in their opening lines, presumably because it is through the three Persons—Creator, Redeemer, and Comforter—that the plan is to be fulfilled. (God does not always insist on his tripartite nature in the mystery pageants; usually he is simply Deus or else Christ. When he does insist on the point, in the Wakefield Noah pageant, for example, or in the *Secunda Pastorum,* it is worthwhile to ask why.) The opening of the Creation pageants must surely be traditional, not the independent discovery of several ingenious poets. Yet it is not traditional in the same way as the opening stanza of, say, "The Twa Sisters"; that is, it is not simply copied word for word, with occasional mistakes, from version to version. Each pageant has its own distinct stanza or assortment of stanzas; the borrowed elements do not regularly appear in the same order; and the pageants progress from their common opening in quite different ways. However heavily dependent the poet may be on some earlier version, when he completely recasts the verse, introducing his own meter and stanza, he presumably takes material from his source not simply for convenience but by choice. Needless to say, the artistic consciousness involved in the choice may be a matter of degree and need not greatly concern us. What is chiefly interesting is the extent to which each playwright, working within the established tradition, has managed by accident or design to achieve an effective pageant.

Unfortunately, the Wakefield version is fragmentary, the MS apparently having lost twelve leaves after line 267; hence any statements made about the playwright's artfulness must be tentative. Nevertheless, the pageant has certain features which encourage us to make guesses. For one thing, even without the last twelve leaves, we know that the design of the pageant was unusually ambitious. The series of events normally treated in three or more separate pageants are presented here in a single pageant rich in characters and in scene changes. (The Towneley MS *Creation* covered everything up to the Cain and Abel story; the *Mactacio Abel* is identified in the MS as "*secunda pagina*.") In York, by way of contrast, the same series of events takes six short pageants—the Barkers' Creation and Fall of Lucifer, the Playsterers' Creation to the fifth day, the Cardmakers' Creation of Adam and Eve, the Fullers' Garden of Eden, the Cowpers' Fall of Adam, and the Armourers' Expulsion pageant. The possible explanation that the Wakefield pageant is earlier than other extant pageants and thus has not yet fragmented into numerous more fully elaborated pageants, in accord with Hardin Craig's theory of pageant evolution,[2] is not a likely explanation here. In comparison with other Creation pageants, but not in comparison with such highly wrought pageants as *Mactacio Abel,* the Wakefield Creation play is very long, a fully elaborated work. There are, moreover numerous indications that the Wakefield pageant is a work which could only have been written with sequences like the York and Chester series of Creation pageants in the background. Like the *Mactacio Abel,* in which Cain's hypocrisy, traditional in the mystery pageants, is first transformed to visual image, then shifted to Abel (the good man who seems hypocritical to Cain), the Wakefield Creation pageant rings subtle and interesting changes on pageant tradition.

Another indication that the pageant is relatively late is the precision of its imagery and the colloquial ease of its language. The pageants generally acknowledged to be most fully evolved—that is, those of the York Metrist and the Wakefield Master—replace the abstraction of earlier pageants with a concern for and delight in realistic detail. Though parts of the Wakefield Creation pageant are conventional and abstract (perhaps the remains of a poetic reviser's source), others have the vividness (sometimes borrowed from a source) of late, realistic pageant style. A fallen devil says:

> We, that were angels so fare,
> and sat so hie aboue the ayere,
> Now ar we waxen blak as any coyll,
> and vgly, tatyrd as a foyll.

> (134–37)

(The image "black as any coyll" occurs in early lyrics and in *Purity,* hence may be considered stock.) Later, Adam says in wonder, exploring Eden:

here ar well moo then we have seen,
Gresys, and othere small floures,
that smell full swete, of seyr coloures.

(237–39)

What all this suggests, I think, is that the mostly lost Creation
play from the Towneley MS was a late, sophisticated work which
some relatively skillful poet put together out of older materials,
adding new devices of his own, exactly as the Wakefield Master revised such pageants as the Ur-*Mactacio Abel*. As for the older materials, it will be sufficient here simply to suggest the close relationship
of the Wakefield pageant to other Creation pageants by a sample
of parallels in phrasing. As for the dramatic strategy of the Wakefield poet, the best approach may be through comparison of his
work with the method of the York poet, whose handling of the
material is traditional.

The Wakefield opening line, "Ego sum alpha et o," has close parallels in all the pageants, within the first line of the first stanza
in the Hegge play, and in nonstanzaic preliminary speeches in Chester and York (in the latter, God says, before the first stanza of verse,
"Ego sum Alpha et O. vita via / Veritas primus et nouissimus").
With the third and fourth lines of the Wakefield pageant, compare
Chester, line 13. With Wakefield, line 7, compare Hegge, lines 27–28,
and with Wakefield, line 9, compare Chester, line 17. With the
boasts of God, lines 13sq., in Wakefield, compare Chester, lines
85sq. Parallels of this kind can be found throughout all the plays,
along with larger structural parallels—the interspersed singing of the
angels, the dialogue of devils in hell, and so forth.

There is another, more interesting class of parallels between lines
in the Wakefield pageant and lines elsewhere. In Lucifer's first
speech in the Wakefield play, Lucifer repeatedly speaks lines which
are elsewhere given to God. For example, line 81 in the Wakefield
parallels lines 40sq. in the Hegge play (compare Chester, 75sq.) and
lines 83–84 recall lines spoken by God in Chester (see 10 and 95sq.).

What seems to be involved here is a recasting of traditional materials in pursuit of an aesthetic value missing in the earlier plays,
decorum. In the Chester and Hegge plays, God does not simply state
the facts about himself, but rather indecorously talks of his virtues.
The same happens, to a lesser extent, in the York play. God begins by
saying,

> I am gracyus and grete, god withoutyn begynnyng,
> I am maker vnmade, all mighte es in me,
> I am lyfe and way vnto welth wynnyng,
> I am formaste and fyrste, als I byd sall it be.
> My blyssyng o ble sall be blendyng,
> And heldand fro harme to be hydande,
> My body in blys ay abydande
> Vne [n]dande withoutyn any endyng.
>
>   (1–8)

When the York God decides to create a fine place for himself, he gives as his grounds for doing so his great worth: "Sen I am maker vnmade, and moste so of mighte" (9), etc. He then turns to the work of creation, first fashioning Lucifer, and commenting on Lucifer's great beauty and high station, "master and merour of my mighte" (34). All this, if we assume a magnificent stage or wagon and a lofty style of action, can make good theater; the lack of dramatic decorum need not be offensive. But good or bad, it is the traditional base on which the Wakefield poet builds his own special effects.

The Wakefield God introduces himself in flat statements of fact. Even the last three lines of the first stanza are flat when compared to God's statements about himself in other plays. He describes himself here as

> Meruelus, of myght most,
> ffader, & son, & holy goost,
>   On God in trinyte.
>
>   (4–6)

In the third stanza he announces that all that can exist is in his providential sight and that he intends to create and maintain the universe. He begins work immediately, still in flat statements of fact, establishing light and darkness, earth and water, plants, and so on. The first direct praise of God comes not from God himself but in the song of the cherubim, after the work of the fifth day. The praise here is closely parallel to that given to God in the analogous angels' song in the York play and elsewhere. Like the York angels' song, the Wakefield song begins with celebration of God's goodness—his kindness of "mercy" and his love—(York, 41–48; Wakefield 61–66), then turns to celebration of God's creation of Lucifer, sung by Lucifer himself in the York play (49–56), sung by lesser angels in the Wake-

field play (67–76). No mention of Lucifer has been made in the
Wakefield play up to this point: the cherubim select for special
praise what was, for God, merely another fine creation. In the York
play, God himself first called attention to Lucifer's special beauty and
exalted station:

> Of all þe mightes I haue made moste nexte after me,
> I make þe als master and merour of my mighte,
> I beelde þe here baynely in blys for to be,
> I name þe for Lucifer, als berar of lyghte.
> No thyng here sall þe be derand,
> In his blis sall be ȝhour beeldyng,
> And haue al welth in ȝoure weledyng,
> Ay whils ȝhe ar buxumly berande.
>
> (33–40)

From Lucifer's self-praise to his fall, the York playwright develops
his largely static material for thirty-nine lines (57–96). The Wakefield playwright uses another, dramatically more effective strategy.
After the angels' praise, Lucifer begins praising himself—in language
more appropriate to God's legitimate claims and largely borrowed
from Deus speeches in earlier Creation plays. In other words, like
the Pharoah, Herod, and Pilate of later Wakefield pageants—and like
Satan in the Harrowing of Hell—Lucifer in the Wakefield Creation
(and only in this cycle) is dramatically parodic of God. Lucifer says,
for instance:

> If that ye will behold me right,
>   this mastre longys to me.
> I am so fare and bright,
> Of me commys all this light,
>   this gam and all this gle;
> Agans my grete myght
>   may [no] thyng stand [ne] be.
>
> (80–86)

And:

> ffor I am lord of blis,
> ouer all this warld, I-wis,
>   My myrth is most of all;
> the[r] for my will is this,
>   master ye shall me call.

> And ye shall se, full sone onone,
> How that me semys to sit in throne
>   as kyng of blis . . .

(94–101)

Just as in the earlier plays the angels praise God after his boasting speeches and his creation, angels now, in the Wakefield version, praise Lucifer.

> Thou art so fayre vnto my syght,
> thou semys well to sytt on hight;
> So thynke me that thou doyse.

(108–10)

Wiser angels object, introducing a dramatic note missing in this section of the earlier plays. The two sides (good and bad angels) argue, and Lucifer, to prove his power—or perhaps from simple high spirits—says he will "take a flight."

According to George England, something is missing from the Towneley MS at this point. "A scribe has mistaken Lucifer's boastful flight for his fall," England writes. "One or more stanzas containing either a speech of Deus (cp. *Chester* and *Coventry Plays*) or the exclamations of the devils as they fall (cp. *York Plays*) must have been omitted."[3] But the point is by no means certain. What may be involved is ironic, quick transition of a kind seen frequently in the Wakefield plays—in the Jacob play, for instance, at line 84, and in all the famous plays regularly attributed to the Wakefield Master. At all events, by giving the traditional boastful speeches of Deus to Lucifer, from whom boasting is to be expected since he is the original type of pride, and by removing these speeches from his characterization of Deus, the playwright has already implied the fall, which therefore need not be verbally presented. Theatrically he flies and falls, like Icarus.

From this point on, comparison of the York version and the Towneley MS version is not very fruitful, since the plays diverge here, one moving into its conclusion, the other setting up a new episode, God's creation of Eden and man. The York play concludes with complementary angel songs—first the lament of Lucifer and the fallen angels, then the song of praise by the unfallen angels. If the Towneley MS playwright borrowed this contrast, he altered it to suit his purpose. He gives the laments of the first two demons, then turns to God's creation of man, setting the joys of the earthly para-

dise in counterpoise with the sorrows of hell. The structural parallel
—from woe to joy, in each case—is superficial, however. The York
poet's concern is with lively drama, realism. One devil complains
that "oure fode es but filth, we fynde vs beforn" (York, 106); Lucifer,
accused of causing it all, whines that he only "sayde but a thoghte"
(114); and as they debate Lucifer exclaims "lurdans, ʒhe smore me
in smoke" (117). The whole scene, black comedy, ends in a fistfight.
The structurally parallel scene in the Towneley MS version is solemn, dignified. Lucifer himself does not speak; we hear only two
fallen angels who lament with him and for him, the second angel's
final lines lyrically echoing the first angel's last lines. There is no
fight, needless to say; and the theme of the laments is explicit (as
is not the case in the York version):

> We were in myrth and Ioy enoghe
> When Lucifer to pride drogh.
> Alas, we may warrie wikkyd pride,
> so may ye all that standys be side. . . .

$$(154-57)$$

The scene of contrasting emotion, God's speech on earth, ironically
echoes the fallen angels' lament. Adam will have the "Myrth and
Ioy" (177) the angels lost, and whereas they "mon haue payne that
neuer shall stynt" (161), Adam and Eve are "euer more to be in
blis" (190).

This neat thematic control extends to all we have of the Towneley MS version. The pageant's first principle of organization is the
pride theme; its principle of profluence is regular movement from
God's statement of premises to contrasting scenes of joy and grief,
results of acceptance or rejection of God's rules; and the pageant's
chief device for focusing this material is verbal repetition. God's
flat statements in his opening speech set out the reasons for his mastery (omnipotence) and establish his kindness, the blessing love which
creates "water to norish the fysh" and "erth to norish bestys crepe-
and" (55–56). The cherubim's song establishes the right relationship
of creatures to such a God: "Myrth and lovyng be to the, / Myrth
and lovyng over al thyng" (62–63) and focus verbally on "Myrth"
and on "Ioy that neuer shall mys" (66). The imagistic focus of the
song is on light, especially that of Lucifer (68sq.). Lucifer's speech
(77sq.)—much of it, as we have said, ironically borrowed from earlier Deus speeches and all of it appropriate to God, not a creature—

focuses on light (78–79, 82–83), on seeming omnipotence (81, 85–86, etc.), and on mirth and joy (84, 94–96, etc.). In this speech it is emphatically because of his essential joy, not just because of his great power, that Lucifer claims mastery:

> ffor I am lord of blis,
> ouer all this warld, I-wis,
>   My myrth is most of all;
> the[r]for my will is this
>   master ye shall me call.
>
> (94–98)

The solemnity of the fallen angels' laments in hell—the opening cry is "Alas, alas, and wele-wo!" (132); compare the more bellicose York cry, "Owte owte! harrowe!" (97)—insists dramatically on the sorrow which contrasts with the joy of the obedient; and the focus of the laments is on 1) the loss of light (136–37, 140, etc.) and 2) the loss of joy (147–51, 154, etc.).

The next structural block of the play, God's creation of animals and man—a structural block directly parallel to God's first speech—focuses on the power given to man (17sq.), delegated power parallel to God's own in the first speech. As the first speech concluded with proofs of God's kindness, his speech here concludes with proofs of his love for man—proofs given in a phrase which echoes the earlier phrase: "wax in my blissyng" (191), recalling the phrase "In my blyssyng, wax . . ." (59). As the cherubim earlier entered to sing God's praises for the creation of heaven and earth, they enter now to sing his praises for his new creation, and as they earlier praised Lucifer's beauty they now praise Adam and Eve, adding, however, a warning about proud disobedience. Then Adam and Eve praise God in speeches focusing on joy and endless bliss. The scene shifts to hell and Lucifer talks of "so mych wo" (252). He again regrets his pride and then, because he and his fellows have lost joy forever (261) whereas man has "blis withoutten end" (263), he plots man's overthrow. Here the play breaks off.

There are none of the more usual signs that the Wakefield Master had a hand in the writing of his play—there is no trace of his randy language, no hint of his characteristic delight in typology, social criticism, or detailed characterization, and no occurrence of the stanza form which has come to be viewed as his signature—but it seems clear that the man who wrote the Towneley MS *Creation* pageant was a master craftsman. It seems clear, too, that the pageant looks forward to later pageants in this cycle. Lucifer's borrowing of language more appropriate to God, in effect his parody of God, looks forward to the similar parodic treatment of Satanic figures like Herod, "King of Kings," and the unique Wakefield Pilate. Thus the Creation pageant in the Wakefield cycle sets up the focal agon of the cycle as a whole, a battle of the true God and Lucifer-Satan, the cosmic pretender.

TWO

Theme and Irony
in the *Mactacio Abel*

Whatever the pageant may have seemed to its immediate audience, to modern critics the Wakefield *Mactacio Abel* has frequently seemed interesting for its realism but not especially successful either as drama or as dramatic sermon.[1] Eleanor Prosser goes so far as to say,

> Doctrine remains in this play only by sufferance. But even apart from homiletic considerations, the play is unsuccessful. It has no unity: it leaps from farce to Scripture to farce with neither transition nor dramatic probability. The conflict is poorly established (witness the weakness of Abel and God); the characterization is one-dimensional; motivations are inconsistent (Cain's despair); much of the humor is pointless and simple-minded (Cain's striking Pyke-harnes without motivation, just to keep his hand in, or the repeated obscenities that are comic solely by reason of their obscenity); the main interest in the play is irrelevant to the main plot action.[2]

But the pageant is better made than has generally been noticed. What we need to see, here as elsewhere in the work of the Wakefield Master,[3] is that the theme of the pageant may have only distant relationship to the theme shared by other mystery pageants on the same subject, and that the poet's chief means of developing his theme is dramatic irony, often irony grounded in symbolism.

Let us begin by looking briefly at the common theme of the earlier pageants and at the Wakefield poet's departure from convention.

The early Cain pageants take as their theme the place of sacrifice within the scheme of Christian redemption, and they develop this theme mainly in terms of a simple appearance-reality contrast: Cain is presented as a hypocrite who at first seems better than he is, Abel as a true Christian who at first seems less admirable than he is. In the Cornish *Origo Mundi,* Cain eagerly accepts his father's charge that he and Abel make sacrifice to God, but when Cain rushes off at once and Abel pauses to ask the blessing of his father and mother, the audience sees that Cain is less virtuous than he seems. In the Chester *Creation,* Cain's apparent virtue is sustained longer and the process of our gradual recognition of Cain's real nature is more subtle: after hearing his mother's speech on sin, Cain voluntarily chooses to sacrifice; and he is apparently obedient and dutiful, for at his father's command he has tilled the soil and raised a great crop, a fitting portion of which he plans to return to God. But Cain's purpose is impure: he will sacrifice in order to get God to send more; and, whereas the Cain of the *Origo Mundi* offers only a partial sacrifice, the Chester Cain, like the Wakefield Cain, offers only the rotten waste. In both the Cornish and Chester pageants the murder of Abel is more or less well motivated, and the effect upon Cain is despair and therefore, by conventional anachronism, damnation. The focus in all the pageants, early or late, is on Cain, for these pageants, if they are sermons, are hellfire sermons. As an exegetical figure of the disloyal Christian (the basis of the conventional anachronism), Cain is a dramatic warning for imperfect Christians in the audience.

In a later Cain pageant, the York VII, *Sacrificium Cayme and Abell,* Cain is no longer a hypocrite but merely a bully. The murder (which takes place somewhere on one of the missing leaves of the manuscript) is apparently motivated mainly by Cain's bad temper, not by the understandable frustration of the man who thought himself good, as in the Chester pageant. As far as one can tell, given the state of the manuscript, the comic material functions mainly as entertainment; but it must be added that the symbolic structure of the Wakefield pageant is implicit in the York pageant—if the plowboy Brewbarret (Strife-brewer) is not, as the York MS seems to show, a sixteenth-century innovation, a borrowing from Wakefield.

The Wakefield *Mactacio Abel,* like the early Cain pageants, depends on an appearance-reality contrast, as we shall see, but the contrast here is more bold than any seen heretofore; and the pageant is still more unusual in that it takes as its theme not simply sacri-

fice in the scheme of redemption but something much larger, what
the *Pearl*-poet might call the "courtesy" of all lord-vassal relationships, both social and metaphysical. The poet focuses on Cain's relationship to his team, his servant, his brother, his parents, his
church and state, and, finally, to God and the devil; and the poet
alludes in passing to further social and metaphysical relationships—
Nature and God, landowner and tenant, beggar and community,
borrower and lender, priest and congregation. Throughout the pageant, moreover, language and stage business summon up the scheme
of feudalism both here on earth and between earth and heaven.

The poet accepts as his premise the commonplace view that God
and Satan are opposing "lords," one omnipotent, one not, each having his hierarchy of vassals,[4] and he develops his theme in terms of
ironic contrasts, the most important being between Abel, a loyal
vassal of God, and Cain, a false vassal of God and thus, by default,
a true vassal of the devil (drawn from Augustine's notion of the
Body of Christ and the Body of the Devil). A second premise in the
pageant, and the basis of the contrast between Abel and Cain, is
that the feudal interdependence of all stations within the scheme of
plenitude is based upon the love of lord for vassal and vassal for
lord (as Abel knows), not upon obligation, or debt. The poet establishes in dramatic form the relationship between man's feudal commitment to God, the mutual commitments of lords and vassals within
the human community (both ecclesiastical and temporal), and man's
commitment as lord of Nature. The pageant is thus not only religious
but also social. To recognize the theme of the pageant is to see the
significance of Cain's despair: despair is the inevitable effect of Cain's
original substitution of the law of debt for the law of love. Having
murdered Abel, Cain becomes God's debtor; and in terms of Cain's
own mode of action, a mode which Cain projects onto God, it is
useless to ask for mercy. Ironically, Cain is held to a debt of which
God might have quit him, and he pays with eternal torment.

Before turning from this general discussion of theme in the *Mactacio Abel* to discussion of the symbolic and ironic techniques used
in developing it, it may be well to comment on other treatments of
this theme in Middle English poetry, both for the sake of clarifying
what is involved in the conflict between love and power as principles of order and also for the sake of suggesting the centrality of
this theme in medieval English thought.

In Middle English literature the theme of feudal interdependence
is particularly common in courtly or sophisticated poetry. The debate

in *Pearl* is rooted in the question whether the principle of order in the universe is love or power: if love is supreme (as the Pearl says it is), then selflessness and concern for others should inform behavior, and God's grace—or the lady's, or the king's—should be one's plea; if power is supreme on the other hand (as the Jeweler is sometimes inclined to think), selfishness, defiance, or tyranny, depending upon one's circumstances, should inform behavior, and one should plead one's rights. In *Purity* the poet treats love as emulation of the beloved. As one wins a lady by becoming as much like her as possible, the poet says, so one wins God by becoming as much like Him— that is, as pure—as possible. Here the poet sees the failure to emulate as, depending on the nature of the failure, either a mark of disrespect or a proof of scorn. In this poem, selflessness and concern for the other (God, one's fellow man, and Nature) are shown to give power, while the failure to love draws the power of heaven down on one's head, either in the form of moderate punishment (for simple disloyalty—a failure of feudal "patience") or in the form of wrathful punishment (for scorn of God, man, and Nature). The lesson Jonah learns in *Patience* is that God is all-powerful but that, as God explains at the end of the poem, if power were not ruled by love it would result in total annihilation of the universe. Sir Gawain's mistake, read in terms of this scheme, is his wish to both have and eat his cake: a servant of Christ and the Virgin, an emulator and thus "lover" of Christ (mentioned in the poem as the best of knights), Gawain accepts a supposedly magic girdle in hopes of drawing to himself power independent of God's love.

The same argument on power and love as principles of order— or wilfulness vs. selfless love as bases of behavior—is one motif in Chaucer's *Troilus and Criseyde*: throughout the poem Troilus periodically defies or rails against the power of the gods (they cannot make him love against his will, he says; and when they do this and more he accuses them of depriving men of freedom); he at other points slides into the persuasion that love is supreme. A similar argument, this time in terms of more or less selfish masculine and feminine power vs. the love between husband and wife informs the "Marriage Group" if we read the group as does Kittredge. The same argument determines the progress from best to worst in the three eagles' speeches in *Parlement of Foules*, the first eagle claiming selflessness and asking grace, the second claiming his rights and appealing to obligation, the third appealing to the self-interest of the

formel. The argument also receives comment in the lecture on courtesy which Alceste delivers to the comic God of Love (Prologue F)
in the *Legend of Good Women*. The love vs. power debate provides
the point of departure for Gower's *Confessio Amantis* (in the poet's
lecture on kingship) and underlies Langland's views on pride and
the concept of Do-Best. It receives the attention, incidentally, of
every Church authority from Augustine forward and is of course central to Boethius's doctrine of freedom. And the most cursory exami-
nation of, say, Ganshof's study of feudalism reveals that the practical
conflict between the idea of love (or feudal interdependence) as the
basis of order and the idea of power as the basis of order accounts
for every important change in feudal terminology and ritual up to
the decline of the system.[5]

The Wakefield Master's theme in the *Mactacio Abel* (and elsewhere) was, then, common enough; it is unusual only within the
mystery-play tradition, which is in general more narrowly religious.
If it should be objected that the poet's audience was not sufficiently
sophisticated to understand a dramatic treatment of the debate of
love vs. power, it would be in order to observe that however naive
the audience may have been, it lived in a world still deeply conscious
of its feudal heritage. It knew at least in a general way that there
were good masters and bad, as well as good servants and bad, and
it knew that the best kind of tenantry, apprenticeship, or servitude
was that in which owner and tenant, master and apprentice, master
and man were bound not by mutual indebtedness or lawful power
but by affection and mutual interest. The vassal who paid his fee
or did his work grudgingly, or the lord, on the other hand, who
took advantage of his position ("thyse gentlery-men" in *Secunda
Pastorum*) was at best a nuisance. The audience could scarcely help
seeing at once that Cain is both a bad lord and a bad vassal. On
one hand, he mistreats his team, mistreats his plowboy, hurls at his
brother phrases normally used only to one's servants, and denies any
involvement in the welfare of his community; on the other hand,
he defies the authority of parents, church, state, and God.

The poet's symbolic technique was equally conventional, but here
too the main tradition behind him was not that of the early mystery
pageant or its near relative, the allegory of the Mass. The poet's
technique, allegory on a realistic base, looks for precedents to allegory of the sort found in the work of the Gawain-poet, Langland,
Chaucer (sometimes), and an occasional popular lyric. Whether or

not the audience knew Ambrose's *De Cain et Abel*,[6] the Wakefield Master could undoubtedly assume in his audience a knowledge of scripture, which was read to them, explained to them, and allegorized for them Sunday after Sunday. Presenting hard-working but selfish Cain as a plowman, the poet could assume in his audience familiarity with the idea of the plowman as a figure of the assiduous Christian, an equation emphasized in Gregory's *Pastoral Care*. This is not to say that every time a medieval man saw a plowman at work or read of a plowman in a book he thought, "Symbol of the assiduous Christian!" But it took only the most subtle suggestions in a religious play to recall the traditional associations to the audience's mind.[7] The audience was undoubtedly familiar, too, with smoke and stench as emblems of hell,[8] with Cain as type of the false Christian, and with the commonplace identification of tithing (i.e., sacrifice) and paying one's taxes or rent to one's temporal lord. Finally, it is safe to say that most of the Wakefield Master's audience were fairly sure that actual devil's agents appeared among men from time to time, "passing" men, as the Canon's Yeoman would say, who seem mortals but are really fiends. This audience, then, should have no trouble understanding the *Mactacio Abel*.

The central symbolic device in the play, and the root of the poet's dramatic irony, is the character Garcio. As we learn in the opening lines of the play, Garcio is a servant full of his own importance. His at once arrogant and impish commands to the audience and his scurrilous threats are of a sort the audience was probably all too familiar with in everyday life.[9] But I suggest that Garcio's mighty lord is not in fact Cain—or at all events not *only* Cain: Garcio serves the devil. He says:

> Gedlyngys, I am a full grete wat.
> A good yoman my master hat:
> Full well ye all hym ken.
> Begyn he with you for to stryfe,
> Certys, then mon ye neuer thryfe;
> Bot I trow, bi God on life,
> Som of you ar his men.
> But let youre lippis couer youre ten,
> Harlottys euerichoon!
> For if my master com, welcom hym then.
> Farewell, for I am gone.

(14–24)

"You know my master well enough," Garcio tells us slyly. The lines seem pointless with reference to Cain; and if Cain is the master referred to, the lines which follow are hard indeed to explain—first, a sly accusation "Some of you are his men," then a sneering admonition "But let your lips cover your teeth," that is, keep silent and (on a second level of *double entendre*) keep your pointed teeth hidden. Cain's nickname for Garcio, Pikeharnes (steal-armor) can also, on one level, identify Garcio as a fiend, for the identification of Christian virtue and armor is old and common.[10] If it is objected that the identification of Garcio as devil's agent is subtle and would not be caught in the rush of drama, we must recall that it may well seem subtle only because we are forced to deduce everything from the text, not having the production before us. In production, Garcio's identity might be obvious at a glance. There are various possibilities. Since Garcio leaves as Cain comes in, then returns to Cain a moment later, it is conceivable that in early productions of his opening scene Garcio was presented as a devil from head to foot, a creature belched smouldering from the stage entrance to hell, and that when he reappeared he had thrown on a plowboy's sack, a disguise transparent to all but Cain. But no such radical theory is really necessary. The double acting convention speculatively suggested by Professor Swart, in which contrasting styles of acting underscore symbolism—satanic and evil characters acting in one way, good characters acting in another—offers another possible theory of how the poet's meaning was realized in spectacle.[11] Slightly modified, Swart's theory provides an even more likely explanation. Garcio may have been played not simply in the presumably rather general style of any evil character but in the (hypothetical) specific and familiar style of the medieval imp—the style used in the Wakefield Harrowing of Hell and also in the satanic plays of the Wakefield tragic phase, from the *Conspiracio* to the play of the talents. That five-play series, revised by the Wakefield Master—so Pollard thinks, and so I argue in chapter nine, below—may well have given the Wakefield Master his idea for the introduction of an imp figure in *Mactacio Abel*. There too, it may be noted, political and feudal satire may be found, and between the *Mactacio Abel* and the five-play sequence there are also numerous parallels of language and conception.

If we interpret Garcio as a devil's agent, the rest of the play falls into place: with the devil and hell placed directly on stage to watch and smile, the action gains suspense and emotional intensity, and the comedy becomes grimly ironic.

If Garcio is a fiend, Cain's entrance is stinging irony. Garcio has just told devil's men to keep their teeth covered until the devil comes, the master for whom Garcio has prepared the way, and to welcome him at that time. Then, with a flourish, Garcio exits. The farewell signals a new scene, a new entrance, surely that of the devil; but instead there enters a type of the assiduous Christian—Cain driving a plow-team. Obviously, spectacle carries the meaning. The contrast between the apparent Cain and the real Cain, the contrast usual in the older plays, has been transformed into the bolder language of symbolic spectacle. Cain is a devil's man in disguise—though he does not yet know it.

Cain's opening speech proves him a man of wrath. He goads, curses, mocks his animals. The scene is comic, but its function is more ironic than comic, for it identifies Cain as both a false servant and a false lord. His cursing makes it clear that he is not the servant of God that his type as plowman ought to suggest; and his false lordship is established by a fine comic touch: Cain bellows, "What, it semys for me ye stand none aw!" that is, it seems that the animals do not stand in awe of him as servants ought to. (The phrase "stand none aw" has a specifically feudal connotation.) Then Cain shouts, "I say, Donnyng, go fare! / Aha! God gif the soro and care!" Hearing God invoked, the animal instantly leaps forward for fear of God's retribution, though it would not budge for Cain.

Now Garcio returns, and our earlier impression of him as devil is confirmed. The relationship between master and man is quickly established. Garcio is unwilling to work and makes it clear that he feels no respect for his master. Cain says the team's unwillingness to work indicates that they have not been properly fed, and Garcio answers:

> Thare prouand, syr, forthi, I lay beynd thare ars,
> And tyes them fast bi the nekys,
> With many stanys in thare hekys.
>
> (45–47)

More is involved than sass. It is traditional that as God provides for man, man is to provide for the ox.[12] (One recalls, too, Christ's statement that God, like a human father, would not give his hungering child a stone instead of bread.) Garcio ironically reverses all values. Cain is furious, and he strikes his servant. Surprisingly, Garcio strikes back. Cain says, astonished, "I am thi master. Wilt thou fight?" and Garcio replies: "Yai, with the same mesure and weght / That I boro will I qwite" (50–52). The comic surface has, again, its ironic point: here with a vengeance is feudal interdependence based not on love but on debt. Cain waves his servant off in disgust, for there is still the plowing to do; and in an aside the servant defiantly commands the team to stay where it is.

Abel's entrance introduces further ironies. (The ironies which are strictly religious have been treated by Bernbeck; see note 1, above.) We must understand, I think, that Abel is only a boy. From the moment of Abel's entrance we know him an innocent, one uninitiated into evil and, therefore, vulnerable. Consider the scene: Cain and his servant have just exchanged blows, and the servant has defied his master with a joke on mutual obligation. Cain has dismissed the matter because he wants to finish his plowing, but Garcio has told the team to stay put. All servant-lord relationships have broken down (man-God, man-servant, man-Nature) and Garcio and Cain stand glaring as Abel enters. Abel fails to see that there is trouble and greets Cain and Garcio in words which sharply contrast with everything around him: "God, as he both may and can, / Spede the, borther, and thi man" (57). It is a lighthearted, ingenuous speech. Needless to say, both the characteristic gentleness and the affirmation of God's power—an affirmation as natural to Abel as breathing—are significant. Cain snaps:

> Come kys myn ars! Me list not ban;
> As welcom standys theroute.
> Thou shuld haue bide til thou were cald;
> Com nar, and other drife or hald—
> And kys the dwillis toute!
> Go grese thi shepe vnder the toute,
> For that is the moste lefe.
>
> (59–65)

In treating Abel as a servant ("Thou shuld haue bide til thou were cald," etc.), Cain is more or less, though dubiously, within his rights: Abel is a younger brother. But Abel cannot know that Cain has been fighting an ill-fed, cantankerous team and a demonic plowboy, and so to him Cain's scurrilous and domineering fury is inexplicable. Baffled and hurt, Abel exclaims with a gentleness which might restore order in another situation, "Broder, there is none hereaboute / That wold the any grefe" (66–67). The irony is clear: "hereaboute" stands the demonic Garcio.

Abel's mission introduces ironies more grim than any yet found in the play: as Garcio ought to serve Cain, so Cain ought to serve *his* lawful masters—his parents, his country, and God. Refusing to bow to authority, Cain becomes another Garcio, a devil's vassal himself. Abel says, addressing Cain as "Leif brother"—

> It is the custom of oure law,
> All that wyrk as the wise
> Shall worship God with sacrifice.
> Oure fader vs bad, oure fader vs kend,
> That oure tend shuld be brend.
> Com furth, brothere, and let vs gang
> To worship God; we dwell full lang.
> Gif we hym parte of oure fee,
> Corn or catall wheder it be.

(69–77)

His next lines have special point when we recall that Garcio stands watching:

> And therfor, brother, let us weynd,
> And first clens vs from the feynd
> Or we make sacrifice;
> Then blis withoutten end
> Get we for oure seruyce,
>
> Of hym that is oure saulis leche.

(78–83)

Cain mocks his brother as a hypocrite and do-gooder spouting pious sermons:

> How! let furth youre geyse; the fox will preche.
> How long wilt thou me appech
> With thi sermonyng?

(84–86)

The identification of Cain as hypocrite, in the earlier plays, is ironically replaced here by an association of hypocrisy with Abel. The proximity of the smiling Garcio lends force to Abel's advice, however, and Cain's choice of an adage is particularly ironic: The "fox" is, for medieval preachers, alabaster carvers, and book illustrators, the devil himself. Associating Abel with the devil and fearlessly remaining with Garcio (however unwitting the association), Cain dangerously misinterprets his situation.

Cain gives now his reason for not wanting to sacrifice:

> What gifys God the to rose hym so?
> Me gifys he noght bot soro and wo.
>
> (95-96)

The only basis of obligation, Cain says, is debt, and I am not in God's debt: He gives me nothing. But as Abel sees, God gives Cain all his "lifyng" (98)—both his livelihood and life itself. Again Cain insists on the concept of debt: The gift imposes no obligation because Cain never asked for it. He says, "Yit boroed I neuer a farthyng / Of hym—here my hand" (98-99). (Cf. Garcio's joke earlier, "That I boro will I qwite.") The phrase "here my hand" may indicate, as other readers have supposed, that Cain strikes Abel. But it may mean, in addition, "I swear it," an idea derived from hand symbolism in feudal commendations.[13] Abel appeals to authority—Our elders have taught us to sacrifice—but the appeal is useless, for Cain scorns all stations, assuming that no one is more loyal than he is himself. Taking "elders" in the religious rather than in the familiar sense, he snaps, "My farthyng is in the preest hand / Syn last tyme I offyrd" (104-5). In the interest of peace, Abel says nothing but "Leif brother, let vs be walk-and . . ." (106).

The line marks a turning point. Cain's wrath is at last somewhat assuaged, and instead of cursing and ranting he answers the boy seriously, even addressing him, without especially thinking about it, as "leif brothere." The truth is that, though he spoke wholly in anger before, Cain really cannot see why he should give up part of his skimpy profit to a lord to whom, as far as he can see, he owes nothing.[14] The shift in tone, brought about by his brother's gentleness and love, seems clear: "Here my trouth" (110)—again the language is feudal. And so the audience could sympathize, though it could not in conscience approve, when Cain declares,

> My wynnyngys ar bot meyn:
> No wonder if that I be leyn.
> Full long till hym I may me meyn,
> For bi hym that me dere boght,
> I traw that he will leyn me noght.
>
> (111-15)

The oath "by hym that me dere boght" is so natural to the medieval
farmer that it has lost all literal meaning; but if the audience is alert
it cannot miss the irony in the juxtaposition of the familiar oath and
the notion that God "well leyn me noght." Abel's mild answer presents the orthodox view of man's debt: "all the good thou has in
wone / Of Godys grace is bot a lone" (116–17), but Cain continues to
argue, rejecting not only his obligation to God but, in a sense, all
obligations. His reason is cogent, on the surface.

> The dwill me spede if I haue hast,
> As long as I may lif,
> To dele my good or gif,
> Ather to God or yit to man,
> Of any good that euer I wan.
> For had I giffen away my goode,
> Then myght I go with a ryffen hood;
> And it is better hold that I haue
> Then go from doore to doore and craue.

(135–43)

It is the logical but antisocial argument that to give up one's goods is
to become a burden on the community. (Ironically, at the end of the
play we will see Cain and Garcio as beggars whose only hope this side
of the grave is the cry "browes, browes to the boy!") Again Abel suggests the power of lawful authority: "I am full ferd that we gat blame"
(145); and again he appeals to filial devotion and also to familial
brotherhood (154–57). Though none of these appeals has much force
for Cain, Cain does at last consent to go, if only to get it over with.
He says, again treating Abel as a servant, not as a brother, "Now
weynd before—ill myght thou spede!— / Syn that we shall algatys go"
(165–66). Abel is naturally surprised that he should be asked to "com
before," like Garcio, and exclaims, "Leif brother, whi sais thou so? /
Bot go we furth both togeder . . ." (167–68). They go to the place of
sacrifice, and Garcio remains where he is, presumably watching.

Abel's sacrifice and Cain's set up another ironic contrast. Abel offers
with his sacrifice an exemplary prayer expressing proper awe, humble
submission to God's will, gratitude, and steadfast loyalty. Cain's prayer
contrasts in every respect.

Abel's interruption of Cain's skinflint counting of the sheaves is
interesting:

> *Abell.* Cam, brother, thou art not God betaght.
> *Cayn.* We! therfor is it that I say
>   I will not deyle my good away.
>
> (211–13)

Abel means "You are not a loyal servant of God" (*betaght*, from OE *betaecan*). Cain's response ironically recalls the old idea of lord or chief as ring-giver dealing out treasures, an idea very commonly associated with God's generosity (cf. *Pearl*, 605–12). Cain is thus subtly identified both with false lordship and false vassalage. The lines which follow are also interesting:

> Bot had I gyffen hym this to teynd
> Then wold thou say he were my freynd;
>
> (214–15)

If the feudal relationship is based on love, Cain thinks, it is love that is bought, not love freely given. And Cain is not in the market. Abel implores his brother to tithe honestly, and the result is another comic touch: Cain sorts with his eyes shut, after which he finds with pleasure, "I teyndyd wonder well bi ges / And so *euen* I laide!" (231–32; my italics). Horrified that his brother should deal so lightheartedly with eternal fire, Abel exclaims, "Came, of God me thynke thou has no drede" (233). But for all Abel's warnings that God can be dangerous, Cain goes on with his worthless sacrifice. In mockery he says,

> Now has he two,
> And for my saull now mot it go;
> But it gos sore agans my will,
> And shal he like full ill.
>
> (253–56)

The worthless tithe does indeed go as a figure of Cain's soul, and God does indeed like it full ill. Abel tries desperately to make Cain see sense, but Cain will not relent. The upshot is symbolic:

> It will not bren for me, I traw.
> Puf! this smoke dos me mych shame—
> Now bren in the dwillys name!
> A! what dwill of hell is it?

> Almost had myne breth beyn dit;
> Had I blawn oone blast more,
> I had beyn choked right thore.
> It stank like the dwill in hell. . . .

(276–84)

Now God, in the figure of an actor on an upper platform, warns Cain that he had better sacrifice properly. Cain scoffs,

> Whi, who is that hob ouer the wall?
> We! who was that that piped so small?
> Com, go we hens, for parels all;
> God is out of hys wit!

(297–300)

Miss Prosser observes, "We can be sure that the laughter was not at Cain but at God. . . . The audience's mind is altered to the reality of the stage setting—any possible 'suspension of disbelief' is broken—and suddenly the scene before them is really very funny."[15] But this is a mistake. When the characters of Samuel Beckett speak of their own actions as actions in a ridiculous, long-winded play we simultaneously recognize that they are right and that their statement is metaphorically true: life is a ridiculous, long-winded play. Similarly, when Cain speaks of God as a hob-ouer-the-wall the audience simultaneously perceives that Cain is right and that he is perilously wrong. We laugh because we understand that the mistake is natural: the play is a metaphor for life. The still small voice—the feeble voice of an actor or the feeble voice of conscience—is seemingly insignificant, indeed ridiculous; but to ignore that voice is to court the disaster which stands mutely before us in the figure of Garcio.

It is equally understandable and equally ironic that Cain should now turn on Abel, eager to blame anyone but himself, that Abel should cry out that *he* is not to blame, and that, enraged by Abel's infuriating rightness, smug or no, Cain should kill his brother. Cain's weapon, as the poet's audience would instantly perceive, is the weapon with which Samson, fighting for the Lord, slew thousands.[16] Cain, fighting on the side of the devil, slays not an enemy host but a defenseless boy.

Perhaps the finest dramatic irony in the play is that which follows the blow: Abel falls; Cain gradually sees that his brother is dead; he refuses to believe it. Cain says: "So. Lig down ther and take thi rest" (326). Then, desperately justifying himself on moral grounds but also recalling to our minds the might of God's vengeance on the wicked, "Thus shall shrewes be chastysed best" (327). The dead Abel cries for vengeance, and Cain, no longer capable of hiding from the truth, sinks to his final depravity, cursing all mankind in the person of the audience. And now at last he trembles.

> Bot now, syn he is broght on slepe,
> Into som hole fayn wold I crepe.
> For ferd I qwake, and can no rede;
> For be I taken, I be bot dede.
> Here will I lig thise fourty dayes,
> And I shew hym that me fyrst rayse.

> (336–401)

He will creep into some hole—the pit of hell, the audience sees (the recollection of Lucifer's pit in the preceding pageant is inescapable). He will hide himself for forty days—the span of God's destruction in Noah's time (and the span of time the wicked angels fall from heaven in *Purity*). And he rejects the raiser of the dead—Christ. He becomes, in short, satanic.

God calls Cain to repentance, but Cain refuses, blasphemes, mocks God's power, and expresses scorn for all mankind. He calls for his servant, and Garcio, who has seen it all, crosses the stage to the place of the murder. Cain strikes Garcio "bot to vse my hand" (393), that is, only to exercise his now totally corrupt mastery. Cain is dramatically presented, at this point, as a figure of the false lord; like Lucifer in the preceding pageant, he looks forward to such tyrant figures as Pharao, Herod, and Pilate, who are defined in this cycle as usurpers of the power which rightly belongs to God. Cain tells Garcio of the murder, and Garcio, feigning astonishment and pious alarm, cries out loudly that he will no longer work for Cain, for fear of the police. Cain hushes Garcio and promises him defense. Ironically, as Professor Cawley has pointed out, Cain twists God's refusal to allow the murderer himself to be murdered (371–73) into a royal proclamation of pardon.[17] Cain instructs his servant to command silence by shouting "Oyes, oyes, oy" (417); but Garcio shouts instead "browes, browes to the boy" (418), like a beggar rather than a servant. Cain's authority is bogus and so Garcio, in his character as mortal, is in fact a servant only in the sense that all man-

kind are a beggar's masters. Garcio ironically mocks the empty
proclamation line by line, exploding (often in exegetical jokes) Cain's
absurd claim of power with the bleak truth that both master and
man are miserable outcasts. When Cain turns on him in fury, Garcio
climbs up out of reach. From his elevated post, an ironical visual
suggestion of the pulpit, he ironically blesses, that is, curses, the
audience.

The play is now over, in a sense; but the characters have to be
gotten off, and the audience has to be left with a sense of the seriousness of Cain's situation, for the powerful drama of the sacrifices
and the murder may be lost behind the black humor of the bogus
proclamation. And so Cain calls Garcio down and Garcio, somewhat surprisingly, comes. Cain warns Garcio that henceforth he had
better step carefully; Garcio leaves, driving the team; and the cosmic
outlaw bids farewell, solemnly enough, to the audience. His farewell
—the last lines of the pageant—is to a world in which degree and
station are still of significance:

> Fare well les, and fare well more!
> For now and euermore
> I will go me to hyde.
>
> *Exit.*

THREE

Christology in the Noah

One level of meaning in the Wakefield *Processus Noe cum Filiis* seems perfectly obvious: as God chastises man for his bad behavior, Noah strives, mostly in vain, to chastise his wife.[1] Anyone in the middle-class or lower-class audience might have understood this. But this overall plan is supported by materials which subtly heighten the central dramatic idea. Chief among these supporting materials is the poet's Christological treatment of Noah. Let us begin, like the pageant, at the beginning.

Noah's opening soliloquy and prayer serve as background to the main event of the play, the flood. The organizing principles embodied in this section and developed through the pageant might be hard to catch in the rush of drama, but for good listeners they need not be unintelligible. Noah's opening words are

> Myghtfull God veray, maker of all that is,
> Thre persons withoutten nay, oone God in endles blis,
> Thou maide both nyght and day, beast, fowle, and fysh;
> All creatures that lif may wroght thou at thi wish,
> As thou wel myght.
> The son, the moyne, verament,
> Thou maide; the firmament;
> The sternes also full feruent,
> To shyne thou maide ful bright.

$(1-9)$

The lines make two important points: God's absolute authority as creator and source of all life (preparing for the third movement's focus on God's just destruction of life), and the harmony of the "Thre persons withoutten nay, oone God in endles blis." The poet's focus on the Trinity of God is not surprising in a mystery pageant; but it should be noted that God's triune nature will be insisted upon throughout this pageant, that the Trinity is not ordinarily mentioned in other Noah pageants, and that elsewhere in the work of the Wakefield Master the Trinity is insisted upon in only a few places, for instance in the *Secunda Pastorum,* where once again God's triune nature is thematically central. These opening lines also introduce light imagery which is to be important later: the sun, the moon, and, most important, the fixed stars "ful feruent," that is, "burning" or "glowing" and also "fervent"—that is, steadfast, loyal.

The star image serves to comment on Lucifer's betrayal of God, presented in the second and third stanzas. Noah says:

> Angels thou maide ful euen, all orders that is,
> To hauve the blis in heuen: this did thou more and les,
> Full mervelus to neuen. Yit was ther vnkyndes
> More bi foldys seuen than I can well expres,
> Forwhi
> Of all angels in brightnes
> God gaf Lucifer most lightnes,
> Yit prowdly he flyt his des.
> And set hym euen hym by.
>
> (10–18)

By juxtaposition to the image of stars "ful bright," and in full accord with the traditional identification of angels as light,[2] the brightness of angels is associated with the brightness of stars. But in contrast to the stars, Lucifer "flyt his des." The idea of Lucifer's brightness is immediately repeated:

> He thoght hymself as worthi as hym that hym made,
> In brightnes, in bewty. . . .
>
> (19–20)

Plunged into hell, Lucifer and his band become, in effect, fixed stars of another sort:

Shall thay *neuer wyn away*
Hence vnto domysday,
Bot *burn* in bayle for ay;
Shall thay neuer dysseuer.

(24–27; my italics)

Formerly unwilling to remain by choice in their appointed place,
they keep their new place because of God's power. Next Noah speaks
of Adam and Eve, and again the idea of harmony versus discord
is central:

Soyne after, that gracyous Lord to his liknes maide man,
That place to be restord, euen as he began;
Of the Trinité *bi accord,* Adam, and Eue that woman,
To multiplie *without discord,* in Paradise put he thaym,
And sithen to both
Gaf in commaundement
On the tre of life to lay no hend. . . .

(27–34; my italics)

Seduced by Lucifer, man is driven from the security and high
station of Eden to a life of woe and uncertainty, a life which contrasts with that of the fixed stars in that it is, in effect, one of
motion, "Fyrst in erth, and sythen in hell"—unless God sends mercy.
The oil of mercy (46), perhaps on one level (as in commentary tradition) a play on the image of oil which quiets troubled waters, will
come if man loves and dreads God; but most men, Noah says, are
engaged in the seven deadly sins (51–54). And so Noah dreads that
God will take vengeance once again. He himself has been steadfast
in the only way dismal fallen man can be. He has lived his long
life "without distance;" that is, he has not stirred about like false
Lucifer, or like wicked man; he is as firm in earth as "any sod"
(58), but he admits by that image his distance from burning stars—
he is "cold / As muk apon mold," and is withering away. He therefore prays that he and his children may be spared and may not, like
the angels and like Adam, "fall" (66).

God's speech in heaven roughly parallels Noah's prayer. He is
man's sovereign, having made earthly authorities—dukes, emperors,
and kings—with his own hand; man should therefore, like the fixed
stars, be "full feruent" (77). Here fervor takes on a new connota-

tion. "Man must luf me paramoure" (80) God says, and: "Me
thoght I shewed man luf when I made hym to be / All angels
abuf . . ." (82–83). Whereas Noah's emphasis has been on the creature's debt to power, God's emphasis is on the creature's debt to both
power (as creator of earthly powers) and divine love. Accord is thus
not simply obedience, a negative quality, but also the positive quality, love. Here as in the *Mactacio Abel* God's authority has a double
basis: God is both man's lord and his lover or, in the language of
scriptural typology, bridegroom. Since man sets no store by "his
soferan," God repents having created man; however, since Noah's
family is in accord with him ("thay wold neuer stryfe / With me
then me offend" [107–8]) he will spare them. Again, accord is associated with stasis or firmness like that of the fixed stars, and discord is identified with motion. "In erth," God says "I se bot syn
reynand to and fro" (111; my italics). He will overcome this turbu-
lence of sin "With floodys that shall floo" (115), another, more terrible motion. He descends to tell Noah his plan, orders him to build
the ark, and tells Noah his thematically significant name: "Oone
God in Trynyty" (169).

The remainder of the pageant's first movement is conventional
except for occasional departures which serve to keep the central
ideas, accord and discord, in focus. As in other versions of the Noah
story, God makes a point of the fact that Noah

> was alway well-wirkand, to me trew as stele,
> To my bydyng obediand; frendship shal thou fele
> To mede.
>
> (120–22)

But it is the Wakefield poet's thematic concern with harmony which
explains the introduction of such new details as "Look no man the
mar" (129) and "With the shal no man fyght, nor do the no kyn
wrake" (138).

In the second movement of the pageant the feudal and love-rela-
tionships of God and man have their human, hence comic, reflection: as man fails to love and obey God, *Uxor* fails to love and obey
Noah, the proper authority within the family; and as God smites
man for failing to love and obey, Noah (departing from God's instructions at lines 129 and 138) makes a valiant attempt at smiting
his wife. Much of the comedy of this movement is obvious to any
audience, but some of it involves an ingenious kind of play with

religious concepts no longer widely current. Here as in the commentaries and in the alliterative *Purity,* Noah is a type or presignification of Christ; the ark is a type of the church; the Flood adumbrates the Last Judgment and at the same time looks back to the Fall.

Most if not all of the Christian typology in the play is traditional. Richard Rolle says of the loyal and pure Christian, "And þan þou comes intil swilk rest and pees in sawle, and quiete withowten thoghtes of vanitese [or] of vices, als þou war in sylence and slepe and settle in Noe schyppe. . . ."[3] The *Purity*-poet, as I have shown elsewhere, offers an elaborate interpretation in which the ark represents not only the elevated church or Second Paradise but also the First Paradise (Eden) and its anagogical signification, the Body of Man.[4] Hugh of St. Victor offers an elaborate reading in *De Arca Noe Morali et Mystica.* The best known account is that of Augustine in the *City of God.* The ark, he says,

> is certainly a figure of the city of God sojourning in this
> world; that is to say, of the church, which is rescued by the
> wood on which hung the Mediator of God and man, the
> man Christ Jesus. (1 Tim. ii.5) For even its very dimensions,
> in length, breadth, and height, represent the human body in
> which He came. . . . And its having a door made in the
> side of it certainly signified the wound which was made
> when the side of the Crucified was pierced with the spear:
> for by this those who came to Him enter. . . .[5]

I do not mean that one can interpret the pageant simply by reading all the commentaries. Medieval exegetes work out the story in various ways, some emphasizing one detail, some emphasizing another. For instance, Noah's wife may be treated as a type of the Virgin or as a type of Eve, her emblematic antithesis.[6] The possible hypothesis that medieval audiences expected traditional typology in the mystery plays would fail to do justice to the Wakefield Master's feeling for structure and would fail to account for the striking difference between the comic section of the York *Fishers and Mariners'* pageant, where no puns like the Wakefield poet's can be found.

The Wakefield poet's method is not simple allegory in which Noah equals Christ. Noah is a man, at once typic of Christ and, in his mere humanness, comically unlike the Savior he foreshadows. Whereas Christ is omnipotent lord of His bride, the church or fellowship of Christians, Noah shudders to think what his wife will say and do to him when he tells her he has to build an ark. When he finds her, Noah says timidly, affecting a cheerfulness he knows will not really save him from her wrath: "God spede, dere wife! How fayre ye?" (190) She snaps:

> Now, as euer myght I thryfe, the wars I the see.
> Do tell me belife, where has thou thus long be?
> To dede may we dryfe, or lif, for the,
> For want.
> When we swete or swynk,
> Thou dos what thou thynk,
> Yit of mete and of drynk
> Haue we veray skant.
>
> (191–98)

Double entendres fall thick and fast. The phrase as *euer myght I thryfe* possibly refers, here as sometimes in Chaucer, to "thriving" in the special sense of living on; but *the wars I the see* plays on "seeing God with [one's] eyes"—the running refrain in *Purity* and a common medieval locution (as in "as I hope to see God"). Uxor's "where has thou thus long be?" plays on the idea of the long wait of man for the Redeemer. It is indeed "for the" (because of Thee) that "To dede may we dryfe, or lif." Uxor's "mete" and "drynk" ironically suggest the bread and wine, body and blood, traditionally associated not only with the Mass but also with the celestial banquet (cf. *Pearl,* line 1064). The lines "When we swete or swynk, / Thou dos what thou thynk" allude to the parable of the vineyard. As the *Pearl*-poet has it,

> "More haf I of ioye and blysse hereinne,
> Of ladyschyp gret and lyueȝ blom,
> þen alle þe wyȝeȝ in þe worlde myȝt wynne
> By þe way of ryȝt to aske dome.
> Wheþer welnygh now I con bygynne—
> In euentyde into þe vyne I come—
> Fyrst of my hyre my Lorde con mynne:
> I watȝ payed anon of al and sum.
> ȝet oþer werne þat toke more tom,
> þat swange and swat for long ȝore,
> þat ȝet of hyre noþynk þay nom,
> Peraunter noȝt schal to-ȝere more."[7]

Noah says, "Wife, we ar hard sted with tythyngys new" (199—that is, New Tidings, the Gospel). But the wife rants on:

> Bot thou were worthi be cled in Stafford blew,
> For thou art alway adred, be it fals or trew.
> Bot God knowes I am led—and that may I rew—
> Full ill;
> For I dar be thi borow,
> From euen vnto morow
> Thou spekys euer of sorrow;
> God send the onys thi fill!
>
> (200–207)

In his typic identification, Noah is worthy to be clad not in Fool's blue, as his wife thinks, but in royal purple; he is dreaded, not dreading; he leads his wife (as Mystical Body) in a way anything but "Full ill;" *he* is *her* surety or "borow," not she his; and he does pay for her sins "From euen vnto morow" in the Crucifixion— a man acquainted with grief (he "spekys euer of sorow") who gets his fill once (the passion). The wife continues:

> We women may wary all ill husbandys;
> I haue oone, bi Mary that lowsyd me of my bandys!
> If he teyn, I must tary, howsoeuer it standys,
> With seymland full sory, wryngand both my handys
> For drede.
>
> (208–12)

On the surface, the phrase "bi Mary that lowsyd me of my bandys!" is simply an oath of sorts, as Cawley glosses it ("Our Lady's bands, confinement at childbirth"); but the line means also "I have one [a husband or Bridegroom] by Mary [he is the Son of Mary] who freed me from my bonds [death]." When Christ is angry, one must tarry (in hell) with a sad face, wringing one's hands. But the wife adds, comically devilish, that at other times she gets her licks in.
    Noah angrily strikes his wife, and she cries out:

> A, so! Mary, thou smytys ill!
> Bot I suppose
> I shal not in thi det
> Flyt of this flett:

> Take the ther a langett
> To tye vp thi hose!
>
> (221–25)

The wife's insubordinate refusal to "Flyt of this flett" still owing
a blow to her husband recalls Lucifer's insubordinate leaving of his
"des" for a place equal to God's "hall in heuen," as Noah has called
it; but God is better than Noah at driving upstarts out. The lines
at the same time recall the parable of the wedding feast, wherein
a man without proper garments and wearing tattered or fallen stock-
ings is hurled out of the great lord's hall into darkness just as the
impure Christian will be cast out of heaven.[8] Here, as in all her
unwitting echoes of scripture, *Uxor* puts herself in the position of
lord and puts Noah in the position of vassal, reversing proper social
order and (allegorically) revising the Christian's relationship to
Christ.

After the dialogue and battle with his wife, Noah goes out to
work on the ark, and here too puns develop the typic identification
of Noah and Christ. A few examples should suffice. "To begyn of
this tree my bonys will I bend," Noah says (253). Compare this with
Christ "bent" on the cross (e.g., in *Pearl*, 813–14). Later Noah says,

> To drife ich a nayll will I not forsake.
> This gere *may neuer fayll,* that dar I vndertake
> Onone.
> This is a nobull gyn:
> *Thise nayles so thay ryn*
> *Thoro more and myn,*
> Thise bordys ichon.
>
> (273–79; my italics)

And again, "This will *euer endure,* therof am I *paide*" (283; my
italics).

The wife's refusal to enter the ark, a traditional element of the
Noah story (as in the York *Fishers and Mariners' Play*) becomes, as
a result of the typology developed throughout, a representation of
late repentance. Noah says, encouraging *Uxor,* "Dame, as it is skill,
here mus vs abide grace" (334—i.e., here in the church we must
await not merely feudal but divine "grace"). But the wife is at-
tracted to what church writers might call false felicity. She says

she will not budge "Till I haue on this hill spon a space / On my rok" (337–38). Perhaps she sits on a parody of Zion, spinning on a parody of the Rock of Salvation, or perhaps the allusion is more complicated. The spinning may allude to Eve's work in Eden, in popular tradition ("When Adam delved and Eve span . . ."), or may allude, more distantly, to the parable of the rich man who gave up all his woolens and linens to buy the pearl of price, figure of the New Jerusalem (of which another figure is the ark). The sacrifice, if this guess is right, is one that *Uxor,* in her unreasoning stubbornness and concupiscence, will not make. More puns (mostly obvious) follow, the rain begins, and *Uxor* runs for the ship. Noah is annoyed by her late entrance. He beats her and she fights back and even wins the round—though she fails to notice that she is on top of him and has won. (He "lies below," as did Christ in death, and unlike Christ he cannot raise himself.) The three sons stop the fight (a comic reversal of the family chain of authority) and the old married couple comes to peaceful terms. So ends the second movement.

The third movement develops, on both the literal and the allegorical levels, the return of harmony. While Noah's wife was holding back from the gangplank, earlier, Noah observed, "the planettys seuen left has thare stall" (345); now, at the beginning of the third movement, *Uxor* says, "I se on the firmament, / Me thynk, the seven starnes" (422–23). Now that God's punishment of the wicked is complete, and now that Noah's comically clumsy punishment of his wife has brought her to submission to his more or less rightful headship,[9] the poet appropriately reintroduces his earlier image of order through faithfulness, the stars in their seven stations.

With God as their "stere-man," or pilot, a pun on "star-man," the family now sails, on the literal level, toward firm ground in the waning flood and, on the allegorical level, toward the salvation Noah earlier prayed for, "thi hall / In heuen." Puns again establish the double meaning of the action. The wife says, "We shuld haue a good feest, were thise floodys flyt" (454), calling up the idea of the feast of the blessed. Again:

Vxor. What grownd may this be?
Noe. The hyllys of Armonye.

(465–66)

Armonye here seems to mean both *Armenia* and *harmony.* The third son's exclamation (525) that the ship stands as "still as a stone" is open to a similar double reading: as still as a stone and as still as the Rock of Salvation.

Accord is reestablished because God has proved his absolute authority and power, overwhelming all overweening pride: "Many castels, I say, / Grete towns of aray" (535–36), the "prowdist of pryde" (543). All that is left is the relatively loyal family of the good vassal, Noah, who prays at the end of the play, much as he prayed near the beginning:

> I pray hym in this space;
> In heven hye with his to purvaye vs a place,
> That we,
> With his santys in sight,
> And his angels bright,
> May com to his light.
> Amen, for charité.

(552–58)

The play has come full circle, the third movement picking up the central imagery of the first (light and motion images and commentary on the fall of the proud) and returning, too, to the elevated tone of the first. The beginning and the end are brought together in terms of spectacle, as well—the figure of Noah praying.

FOUR

Idea and Emotion
in the *Abraham*

The Wakefield *Abraham* has generally been dismissed as a work of no particular interest and certainly no poetic merit. A. W. Pollard, one of the most enthusiastic defenders of the Wakefield pageants, concedes that this one is "very dull." He writes, "The dramatist of the *Abraham* could not fail to attain to some pathos in the treatment of the scene between Isaac and his father; but though he avoids the mistake of the York playwright who represented Isaac as a man of thirty, his handling of the scene is distinctly inferior to that of the Brome Play and the Chester cycle."[1] The judgment is standard.[2]

In one respect the handling of language in the Wakefield version is distinctly superior to that in the analogues. One of the striking devices found in the Wakefield pageants which most clearly shows the Wakefield Master's hand is the distribution of a single verse to two or more speakers, a device which increases the realism and force of dialogue. The Hegge version of the Abraham story contains no broken speeches: characters are always given complete lines, half stanzas, or stanzas. The same is true in the Brome version and in the Chester. Lines are broken in the York version on three occasions, all on exactly the same pattern:

> *Angel:* Abraham! Abraham!
> *Abraham:*   Loo I am here.

The second time Abraham answers "Loo, here I wys," and the third time, "Loo, here in dede." In the Wakefield version such breaking of the lines is common. In the twenty-third stanza, for example, we find:

> *Abraham:* Isaac!
> *Isaac:*   Sir?
> *Abraham:*   Com heder, bid I;
>   Thou shall be dede what so euer betide.
> *Isaac:* A, fader, mercy! mercy!
> *Abraham:* That I say may not be denyde;
>   Take thi dede therfor mekely.
> *Isaac:* A, good sir, abide;
>   ffader!
> *Abraham:*   What, son?
> *Isaac:*   —to do
>   Your will I am redy,
>   Where so euer ye go or ride.

Such line breaking occurs throughout. Interestingly enough, the pageant's shifts from the regular rhyming and tetrameter of the opening stanzas generally correspond with the passages in which lines are distributed to more than one speaker.

It is natural to feel, in the light of all this, that in the Wakefield *Abraham,* as in the *Mactacio Abel,* we have a work revised or adapted by a man worth watching closely, or to put it less coyly, revised by the Wakefield Master. When we scrutinize the various Abraham pageants we find that, in fact, the Wakefield is in most respects the best of the lot.

The Chester pageant[3] is a loosely constructed exposition of the meaning of sacrifice. After a prolix introduction by the players' messenger, it opens with a scene in which various gifts or offerings are exchanged. Abraham, who has just helped his brother in war, gives tithes to God and to the king of his city, Melchisedech; Lot gives gratitude offerings to Abraham, Melchisedech, and God; and Melchisedech gives gifts of thanks to God, then gifts, including bread and wine, to Abraham and Lot. An expositor interrupts the action to explain the typic significance of some of this—the bread and wine "signifieth the new Testament"—and comments on the part played by beast-offerings in "the old lawe." Out of gratitude for the tithe He has been given, God promises to grant Abraham's wish for a son and to make Abraham's seed numerous. He hands down the rule that children of Abraham's line must be circumcised, and the expositor interrupts to explain that circumcision is now replaced by baptism. Then, without transition, God commands that Abraham sacrifice Isaac, and Abraham says he will do so. The remainder of the pageant—thirty-two out of sixty-one stanzas—concerns the sacrifice of Isaac. The emphasis throughout this latter half of the pageant is on two ideas, the faithfulness of Abraham and Isaac and the sorrow they feel. Both ideas are kept in focus by verbal repetition, sometimes incremental repetition of the kind found in the popular ballad. Abraham says he will "fulfill thy Comaundment" (221) and "thy bydding done shall be" (224) and, a moment later, "Godis bydding will I not forsake, / but aye obedyent bee" (235–36); Isaac promises "to doe your bydding mekelie" (238), "your bydding I will not forsake" (246), then again promises "to fulfill your byddinge" (248). The obedience theme rings again and again throughout this section, generally in the same phrases, e.g., lines 251–52, 255–56, 295, 303–4, 306, 311, 315–16, 321, 329, 344, 362–64, 366–67, 382, 397, 406–8, etc. Phrases expressing the grief of Abraham and Isaac are equally numerous and equally close as verbal echoes. For instance, Abraham says, "thou burstes my hart in sunder" (276), "thou breakes my harte even in three" (281), "Harte, if thou wolde breake in three" (405), "Ah, sonne, my harte, if thou wolde breake in three" (413), etc. Minor repetitions of phrase and idea support these hammering repetitions; for example, Isaac asks that his eyes be hidden under a blindfold at lines 337, 385–86, 390–91. And the idea of pleasing those one loves occurs several times: at line 312 and elsewhere, Abraham speaks of pleasing God; Isaac speaks of his wish to please Abraham and asks that any past offenses be forgiven; and Abraham laments the fact that he cannot please his wife (324). The obedience, sorrow, and love themes seem to gel at lines 405sq., where Abraham recognizes that he must either please God or please his own heart. Heart, he says

> thou shalt never master me.
> I will no lenger let for thee,
> my God I may not greeve.

Two angels and God resolve the difficulty, the expositor reappears to explain its figurative significance, and the pageant ends.

Though the Chester Abraham and Isaac pageant cannot be called an artistic success, it is an interesting work. The playwright obviously labored for emotional effects, by hammering home his central themes, by insisting upon the dreadfulness of the proposed sacrifice, and by drawing on every available source of family emotion—not only the emotion of father and son but also that of the mother and the brothers and sisters of Isaac (see 225sq., etc.). And he was evidently concerned with the meaning of the story as well. The first half of the pageant, with its elaborate exchange of gifts and offerings, sets up the norm of harmony and generous repayment which God's test of Abraham seems to disrupt; at the end of the pageant the test is justified and becomes the model for order on earth since the Incarnation. The expositor says:

> By Isaac vnderstand I may
> Ihesu that was obedyent aye,
> his fathers will to worke alway,
> his death to vnderfonge.

(473–76)

The Hegge (or N. Town) pageant[4] is more tightly constructed but less complex than the Chester version. It opens with a scene in which Abraham thanks God for his beloved Isaac, then lectures Isaac, with many loving phrases, on complete obedience to God. The playwright's emphasis throughout is on the interrelationship of love, duty, and reward or payment (blessing or praise), and more often here than in the Chester pageant this complex of ideas receives stylized visual treatment. Abraham at one point shows his love for and command of his son by asking him to turn his face ("sone fayre fare þi fface" [21]) as Abraham will later turn his face to the mountain of sacrifice, and give him a kiss. Isaac responds in language and gesture which show his recognition of duty, his love, and his desire for blessing:

> At ʒoure byddynge ʒour mouthe I kys
> with lowly hert I ʒow pray
> ʒoure fadyrly love lete me nevyr mysse
> but blysse me ʒour chylde both nyght and day.

(25–28)

The Hegge pageant is more schematic than the Chester version (God's blessing = Abraham's, Isaac's duty = Abraham's to God, etc.), and the pageant is in general more spare, more intellectual. Like the Chester poet, the Hegge poet uses verbal repetition, but he normally uses his key words and phrases three or four times, not a dozen. Most important of all, the pageant contains far less sentiment.

When Isaac learns that he must die by God's command he responds
not with grief or horror but with willing submission and a recommendation that his father follow his example (145–60). He does not
ask for a blindfold but, for pity of his father, asks that his father
turn his face away as he strikes (a clever reversal of the face-turning
motif). Abraham's victories in battle and the promise that his seed
will multiply are found not at the beginning of the pageant (cf. the
Chester version) but at the end, where they serve the reward motif.
No direct mention is made of Isaac's typic identification with Christ.
The Hegge version is about half the length of the Chester (264 lines
and 476 lines respectively), has unified plot, and has far more tightly
controlled imagery. Whereas the Chester has structural repetitions
which dilate the action (Abraham twice takes up the fire and gives
Isaac the kindling—stanzas 30 and 31), the Hegge has nothing
of the kind. The Hegge has emotion of the kind expressed by a
stained-glass window; the Chester has sentiment of the sort found
in popular romances and ballads of the day—literary forms reflected
in its meter, its language, and its style of repetition.

The emotion feebly expressed in the Chester pageant is expressed
with more force and better control in the celebrated Brome pageant.[5]
There are numerous signs that the Brome is an adaptation of the
Chester or of, more likely, some close analogue which has since been
lost. There are similarities of phrase: for instance, the oft-echoed
line in the Chester, "thou burstes my hart in sunder" (Chester, 276),
recurs in the Brome:

> Thys chyldes words all to-wond my harte (121)
> A! Lord, my hart brekyth on tweyn (127)
> Thys chyld her brekys my harte on-sonder (152)
> For, i-wys, thow breke my harte on thre (156)
> For my hart was neuer halffe so sore (160)
> My hart ys now soo full of woo (164), etc.

Just how close the two versions are may be seen if we compare
parallel passages. In the Chester:

> If I haue trespassed in any degree,
> with a yard you maye beate me;
> put vp your sword if your will be
> for I am but a Childe.

> (289–92)

In the Brome:

> Yff I haue trespassyd a-gens yow owt,
>   With a yard ye may make me full myld;
> And with yowr scharp sword kyll me nogth,
>   For, i-wys, fader, I am but a chyld.

(169–72)

There are numerous parallels of this kind. Both pageants treat the grief Isaac's mother will feel, both use the blindfold motif, and both make extremely heavy use of verbal repetition, generally the repetition of phrases which both pageants share.

The superiority of the Brome pageant has three main causes. First, the plot is unified; second, the patterns of verbal repetition are infinitely more complex in their interweaving, so that genuine poetic effect is achieved; and, third, the conclusion of the pageant, which treats the feelings of Isaac and Abraham *after* the angel's intervention, makes convincing characters of the father and son. When they have caught the sheep (which Isaac merrily addresses in the language of Isaiah on Christ) and are preparing to sacrifice it instead of Isaac, the dialogue becomes strikingly realistic:

> *Isaac:*
>   And I wyll fast begynne to blowe;
>   Thys fyere schall brene a full good spyd.
>   But, fader, wyll I stowppe downe lowe,
>   Ye wyll not kyll me with yowr sword, I trowe?
> *Abraham:*
>   Noo, har[de]ly, swet son; haue no dred;
>   My mornyng ys past.
> *Isaac:*
>   Ya! but I woold that sword wer in a gled,
>   For, iwys, fader, yt make me full yll agast.

(375–82)

Later, when the sacrifice is over, they talk again of Isaac's fear, and Isaac says with a cheerful shudder,

> Ya! be my feyth, fader, now haue I red,
>   I wos neuer soo afrayd before
>   As I haue byn at yin hyll.

> But, be my feth, fader, I swere
> I wyll neuermore cume there
> But yt be a-gens my wyll.

(413–18)

It should be noted, I think, that the emotion here is far more convincing than anything in the earlier part of the pageant—Abraham's
repeated wringing of his hands, his numerous complaints about the
state of his heart, and so on. The earlier section has lyricism; that
is, it has thickly interwoven verbal repetitions which give elevation
but certainly not realism. If for the purpose of analysis we mentally
discount the lyrical effect—the numerous echoes on, for instance,
"Lord of heuyn," "dere fader," "Fader of heuyn," or "Full wyll and
fyne," "I am full fayn to do yowr bedyng," "To folow yow I am
full fayn," etc. (see lines 105–89)—what remains is lisping sentimen-
tality:

> *Abraham:* Now, Ysaac, my owyne son dere,
>   Wer art thow, chyld? Speke to me.
> *Isaac:*   My fader, swet fader, I am here,
>   And make my preyrys to the Trenyte.

(101–4)

In short, the Brome *Sacrifice of Isaac* is fundamentally a pageant of
emotion. The traditional typic identification is brought over from
the source (it appears mainly in refrain lines also to be found in the
Chester version), but the identification of Isaac and Christ is clearly
less important to the poet—unless, of course, it was meant to be
assumed on Amalarius's grounds or carried by spectacle[6]—than the
pity which can be roused through poetic artifice. And at the end of
the pageant, in place of the Chester expositor who comes to explain
the symbolism, we have in the Brome pageant a Doctor who draws
quite another lesson from the story: We must not struggle against
God's will, and women "that wepe so sorowfully / Whan that hyr
chyldryn dey them froo, / As nater woll and kynd" should learn
to accept God's will and obey his commandments. He concludes—
without drawing the traditional parallel—"Now Jesu, that weryt the
crown of thorne, / Bryng vs all to heuyn blysse!"

The Brome pageant looks forward to later sentimental drama, and
no doubt the reason it has been overrated is that it seems a precursor

to later, supposedly less primitive theater. The York and Wakefield pageants do not look forward so directly to later drama: they represent a highly sophisticated extinct art form, the medieval mystery pageant.

In the York pageant,[7] doctrine and symbolism are all-important. In the first five stanzas Abraham addresses the audience, telling more than they probably care to know about his history—how he was first called Abram, later Abraham, how Sarae's name was changed to Sara, as well as the whole story of his seeming barrenness, his conception of Ishmael, and so forth. None of this is particularly dramatic, though a few striking (thoroughly traditional) images catch the eye, and the self-conscious rhetoric is noteworthy:

> He saide my seede shulde multyplye,
> Lyke to þe gravell of þe see,
> And als þe sternes wer strewed wyde,
> So saide he þat my seede shuld be.
>
> (15–18)

At line sixty-five God's angel breaks in with God's grim command, and the action is underway. In this pageant Isaac is a grown man, not thirty, as Pollard complained, but "Thyrty ȝere and more sum dele" (82), that is, of course, about thirty-three, the age of Christ at the time of the event adumbrated in the Isaac story. The poet justifies his symbolic choice of a thirty-three-year-old Isaac in the development of the action. For instance, Isaac himself suggests that he be bound for the sacrifice. His will is ready, he says, but as for his flesh:

> I knaw myselfe be cours of kynde,
> My flessche for dede will be dredande,
> I am ferde þat ȝe sall fynde
> My force youre forward to withstande.
>
> (209–12)

Abraham's response hints ironically at the Isaac-Christ identification: "To bynde hym þat shuld be my beelde [support]!" (223; cf. 59). The pageant is by no means a play of emotion, but it to some extent works as art. Isaac's arguments to his father, urging him to obey God's command, are more convincing coming from an adult than

from a child; and the conventional detail of the blindfold is altered
to suit Isaac's grown-up courage: he wants the blindfold so that he
will not flinch, making the sacrifice imperfect (lines 285–90). There
is not a trace of simpering burble in the York pageant: the central
characters address each other simply as "Fadir" and "Sone," and
when Abraham tells the audience of his pleasure in Isaac he uses
not hyperbole but litotes: "Gyff I were blythe, who wolde me blame?"
(48). The only use of the word *love* in the pageant is in passages expressing Abraham's love of God (60–64, 309–10); and the phrase
"darlyng dere" occurs only (at 311) when Abraham is talking about
Isaac to himself. Clearly, if the York poet knew the Brome version
he did not like it. His pageant has simple but by no means primitive dignity, a minimum of lyrical artifice, no tenderness (though the
manly love of father and son is obvious), no women, no children.
Sentiment is secondary to thought. Servants are introduced simply
for the purpose of extending the system of lord-vassal relationships:
their few lines all point up the similarity of their position with
respect to Abraham, their master, and Abraham's position with respect to God (or Isaac's to Abraham). The end of the pageant for-
mally balances with the beginning: Abraham and Isaac, leaving the
scene of sacrifice, talk of Isaac's forthcoming marriage and look forward to the future—as in the beginning Abraham reviewed the past
—of Abraham's line.

Now let us turn to the Wakefield *Abraham.*

The relationship of this version to other versions of the Abraham
and Isaac story is impossible to establish with any certainty.[8] The
opening line, "Adonay, thou god veray," echoed at the close of
Abraham's prayer (46), may have been suggested by line 263 of the
York pageant, "Now my grete god, Adonay!"—but considering the
number of pageants which have been lost, such guesses cannot carry
much weight. Like the York pageant, the Wakefield opens with a
long soliloquy by Abraham which, if we discount the misrhymed
seventh stanza, breaks off when a voice cries "Abraham! Abraham!"
from above. The Wakefield version insists by subtle means on the
Isaac-Christ identification, often by the use of phrases found in the
York pageant. For instance, in the York Isaac says: "Here sall no
fawte be foune / To make youre forward faylle" (219–20). And in
the Wakefield, one of Abraham's speeches contains the same scriptural allusion: "But no defawt I faund hym in" (219; cf. John 19:38).
On the other hand, many details in the Wakefield pageant draw

from the tradition of the Chester-Brome group. The Wakefield verbal-repetition pattern on *bidding* and *fulfill*, pointed out earlier, has its close analogue in the Chester pageant (221, 224, 235–36, 238, 246, etc., also pointed out earlier), a pattern expanded in the Brome. The Wakefield rings new changes on the Chester-Brome pattern "thou burstes my hart in sunder;" for example, Abraham says to Isaac, "Thi lufly chere makis my hert glad" (103), but in the next stanza, when Isaac has left him, "Alone, right here in this playn, / Might I speke to myn hart brast" (109–10). We might point out many more parallels between the Wakefield pageant and both the York and the Chester-Brome group. As in York, Abraham is directed to the land of "Visyon," and as the York version speaks of going "ought forthe a towne" (115), Abraham in the Wakefield says he must "weynd furth of towne" (131); yet in the Wakefield, as in the Chester and Brome, Isaac is a child, there is much tender talk, Isaac's mother is mentioned; and as in Brome (but not Chester) the pageant ends with realistic talk of Isaac's fright. Though the dating of all the texts is doubtful, and though lost texts may have played a part in the transmission of material, the likelihood is that the Wakefield is the latest version and that it drew from both York and Brome types. We know that in other cases Wakefield playwrights borrowed from nearby York; and the realism in the Wakefield pageant *before* the sacrifice, missing from the Brome version, argues against transmission from Wakefield to Brome. Finally, the general superiority of the Wakefield version to all others strongly suggests that it came late. This assessment of course concerns only the final, adapted Towneley MS version.

The superiority of the Wakefield *Abraham* resides in the truth and richness of its emotion and the complexity of its thought. Take emotion first. In the Brome pageant, convincing emotion does not appear until after the sacrifice of Isaac has been called off and Isaac, bending to light the fire, has the awful—and very human—thought that perhaps his father will strike him when he is not looking. No one will deny that the emotion is true or that the audience must empathize with—and thus draw nearer to—Isaac; but we might legitimately deny that the realism is appropriate to the subject. Isaac's faith and loyalty are suddenly undercut, now that they do not matter any more, and we wonder where his former lofty sentiments came from. This scene (supposing the Towneley MS playwright knew it) is dropped in the Wakefield version, which moves

directly to the Brome conclusion, in which Isaac tells how frightened he was. The smooth poetic style of the Brome—

> I wos neuer soo afrayd before
>> As I haue byn at yin hyll.
>
> But, be my feth, fader, I swere
> I wyll neuermore cume there
>> But yt be a-gens my wyll
>
> (414–18)

—language which sounds appropriate to Malory's canny Launcelot,
gives way in the Wakefield to colloquial speech (including, by the
way, a favorite word of the Wakefield Master, *nere-hand*): "ffor
ferd, sir, was I nerehand mad" (286; cf. *Secunda Pastorum* 2, 11).
At this point, unluckily, the Towneley MS version breaks off.

Whereas in the Brome pageant emotion prior to the angel's intervention is achieved by the artifice of lyricism, the Wakefield poet
achieves it by realistic means. In Brome, Isaac's mother is used this
way:

> *Isaac:* Now I wold to God my moder were her on this hyll!
>> Sche woold knele for me on both hyr kneys
>>> To save my lyffe.
>
> (173–75)

She is used again later in a way conventional to the popular ballad:

> But, fader, I prey yow euermore,
>> Tell ye my moder no dell;
> Yff sche wost yt, sche wold wepe full sore,
>> For i-wysse, fader, sche lovyt me full wyll.
>>> Goddes blyssyng mot sche haue!
>
> Now for-wyll, my moder so swete!
>> We too be leke no more to mete.
>
> (255–61)

This is good, but it cannot compare with Abraham's soliloquy in the
Wakefield pageant, in which all the arguments against obeying God's
command—including what Isaac's mother will say—rise up to fill the
old man with anguish:

I were leuer than all wardly wyn
 That I had fon hym onys vnkynde,
Bot no defawt I faund hym in:
 I wold be dede for hym, or pynde;
To slo hym thus, I thynk grete syn,
 So rufull wordis I with hym fynd;
I am full wo that we shuld twyn,
 ffor he will neuer oute of my mynd.

What shal I to his moder say?
 ffor "where is he," tyte will she spyr;
If I tell hir, "ron away,"
 hir answere bese belife—"nay, sir!"
And I am ferd hir for to slay;
 I ne wote what I shal say till hir.
he lyys full still ther as he lay,
 ffor to I com, dar he not styr.

(217–32)

We find the same close scrutiny of real emotion in Abraham's decision to raise the knife and strike. In all of the analogues, it should be observed, Abraham thinks out loud for a spell, then for no apparent reason gets on with the sacrifice. One might not notice this—one might dismiss it as mere stage necessity—if it were not for the Wakefield poet's having solved the problem. Abraham discovers that the more he thinks about his grief the worse it gets and so resolves to act at once:

It must nedis be, withoutten lesse,
thof all I carpe on this kyn wise,
The more my sorow it will incres.

(251–53)

He decides to slay Isaac "in a rush"—and it is at this point that, in the nick of time, the angel instead of merely calling out (as in the other versions) *seizes* Abraham, hurling him to the ground and saving Isaac's life. The difference in emotional impact is enormous, though obviously the thing might well go comic if stupidly acted.

But ultimately the emotional force of the pageant is a product, not of the poet's psychological realism, but of his idea concerning the relationships between servant and master, child and father, man and

God. Though the Wakefield pageant contains much tender speech, neither God nor Abraham are entirely gentle fathers: they are loving and just but also stern; and that, the poet seems to suggest, is exactly as it ought to be. (Compare the power-love themes in the Towneley MS *Creation*, the *Mactacio Abel*, and the Noah play.)

Abraham's opening prayer is a plea for mercy framed on the elegaic *ubi sunt* form. "Wheder ar all oure elders went?" Abraham asks (11). He speaks of Adam's fall and sorrow, Cain's murder, the triumphs of Noah, now long gone, and, finally, of his own great age and fear of death. (Like the York opening, the opening prayer here sets the pageant in its relation to others of the cycle, but in this case the summary of events is emotionally relevant. Cf. the opening of the Wakefield Noah play.) In an interpolated stanza God speaks, above, saying that he will help his servant but only "if he be trast" (54) and "trew of louf" (56). He calls down, "Abraham! Abraham!" as in other versions, but only in this version does Abraham answer not "Here I am" but, realistically, "Who is tht? war! let me se! / I herd oone neven my name" (58–59). God gives his seemingly cruel command in language strangely harsh: "And take with the Isaac, thi son, / As a beest to sacryfy" (70–71). Abraham replies with immediate obedience,

> A, lovyd be thou, lord in throne!
> hold ouer me, lord, thy holy hand,
>   ffor certis thi bidyng shall be done.
> Blissyd be that lord in euery land
>   wold viset his seruand thus so soyn.
> ffayn wold I this thyng ordand,
>   ffor it profettis noght to hoyne;
>
> (74–80)

He obeys only because he must—"it profettis noght to hoyne" (delay or, possibly, grieve)—yet his heart is "hevy as leyde" (82). He thinks how frightened Isaac will be when he learns of the command, then calls to him. The child comes to him eagerly, saying, "I luf you mekill, fader dere" (95). Abraham sees the grim irony in it. "And dos thou so?" he asks, reserved. Then, testing, like God, he adds, "I wold wit how / lufis thou me, son, as thou has saide" (96–97). The child's answer has more grim irony for Abraham: "God hold me long youre life in quart!" (100), and the father who lamented in his opening prayer that soon he must depart for hell, like his forefathers, can only answer—in ironic litotes, as in the York play—"Now, who would not be glad that had / A child so lufand as thou art?" He tells Isaac that his "lufly chere" makes his heart glad, but even now he uses no tender expressions. He says simply, "Go home, son; com sone again, / And tell thi moder I com ful fast" (105–6), and then *after* Isaac is out of sight, he releases his grief. When the grief is in control he calls Isaac back with the single word "Isaac!" and Isaac answers, like a well-trained son, "sir!" Abraham gives his commands: they will go to a far country to sacrifice; Isaac will ride, Abraham walk; Isaac is to see that he has any provisions he will need; and at last, softening, Abraham says, "Do make the redy, my darlyng" (138)—his first term of affection. They leave, with servants who function exactly as in the York play, and when finally Isaac asks what beast will be sacrificed, Abraham tells Isaac he is to die.

Here again the poet's eye for realism is unerring and his respect for real human emotion true. Learning that he must die, Isaac cries, "I am hevy and nothyng fayn, / Thus hastely that shall be shent" (175–76) and—*he draws back*. Abraham checks him instantly with the one sharp word, "Isaac!" and again the boy answers, "sir!" Abraham calls his son back to him, and we watch the following taut exchange between the loving but intransigent old man and the baffled, terrified boy:

> *Abraham:*   Com heder, bid I;
>   Thou shal be dede what so euer betide.
> *Isaac:* A, fader, mercy! mercy!
> *Abraham:* That I say may not be denyde;
>   Take thi dede therfor mekely.
> *Isaac:*   A, good sir, abide;
>   ffader!
> *Abraham:*   What, son?
> *Isaac:*   to do youre will I am redy,
>   where so euer ye go or ride,
>   If I may oght ouertake youre will,
>   syn I haue trepa[s]t I wold be bet.
> *Abraham:* Isaac!
> *Isaac:*   What, sir?
> *Abraham:*   good son, be still.
> *Isaac:* ffader!
> *Abraham:*   what, son!
> *Isaac:*   think on thi get!
>   what haue I done?

> *Abraham:*   truly, none ill.
> *Isaac:* And shall be slayn?
> *Abraham:*   so haue I het.
> *Isaac:* sir, what may help?
> *Abraham:*   certis, no skill.
> *Isaac:* I ask mercy.
> *Abraham:*   that may not let.
>
>   (179–92)

The exchange continues, cruelly drawn out to its painful climax: Isaac, finding that his protest "I luf you ay" (209) is of no avail, and mistakenly thinking that his father does not love him as he pretends, tries to plead by his mother's love rather than Abraham's love for him (211). Abraham obviously understands what has happened. He turns away, weeping because "he spekis so rufully to me" (215).

The *raison d'être* for the whole painful scene is that in the Wakefield version—and in no other—Abraham, like God, acts without explaining. There can be no pious and improbable sermons from Isaac to his father on the subject of duty, for Isaac does not know why his father means to kill him. On the contrary, much of the old man's dignity comes from the fact that he controls himself: he does not whimper to God, does not simper to his son, but loves, suffers, obeys. It is fitting, both thematically and dramatically, that the angel who comes in quick obedience to God's command, should stop the sacrifice not simply with words but with sudden violence, that Abraham should react with fear and confusion, and that the angel, bringing mercy, should speak like a stern medieval father:

>   stand vp, now, stand!
>   Thi good will com I to alow,
>   Therfor I byd the hold thi hand.
>
>   (258–60)

The angel points out the entangled beast and gives God's message; Abraham has doubts; the angel dispells them in a short sentence, "I say the yis" (270); and Abraham turns from the angel at once—another brilliant psychological touch—with the surprising words,

>   To speke with the haue I no space,
>   with my dere son till I haue spokyn.
>
>   (273–74)

And the angel withdraws. Father and son are reconciled, Isaac tells how afraid he was, and the pageant breaks off. Since the two pages missing from the manuscript contained almost all of the fragmentary *Isaac* which follows the *Abraham,* we cannot have lost many lines. At all events, the last line we have—"ffor ferd, sir, was I nere-hand mad" —is fitting.

This review of the play suggests that the Wakefield *Abraham,* though it contains no Wakefield stanzas, may well be largely the work of the Wakefield Master. The indications of this are the broken-line dialogue, the realistic portrayal of father and son, the poet's concern with real-life social issues—the order of a well-run family—and occasional words which are favorites of the Wakefield Master, e.g., *nerehand.* In any case, the play fits the larger plan of the Wakefield *Corpus Christi,* in which Christology identifies Old Testament figures with the larger drama of the cycle as a whole, the conflict of Satan and Christ.

F I V E

"Insipid" Pageants:
The Limits of Improvisation

Up to the *Prima Pastorum* of the Wakefield Master, the pageants which follow the Abraham and Isaac play in the Towneley MS are, except for the *Pharao,* relatively dull, if not "insipid"—A. P. Rossiter's word.[1] One might pass over all of them in silence except that the very dullness of most of the group raises questions. Long sections of the Towneley MS contain brilliant writing: the MS begins, we have seen, with what must have been a complex pageant on the Creation and Fall—a late and untypical pageant involving many characters and many scene changes; the MS contains the most sophisticated pageant still extant on Cain and Abel;[2] after this the MS has brilliant pageants on Noah, Abraham, and, later, the Nativity, the Slaughter of Innocents, and the Conspiracy, Trial, Crucifixion, and Resurrection of Christ, the Harrowing of Hell, and the Judgment. In a cycle largely made up of first-rate pageants, some original, some adapted from earlier, cruder pageants, why was this long stretch of dull pageants allowed to stand?

Put it another way. Of the pageants involved—the fragmentary *Isaac,* the *Jacob,* the *Prophetarum, Pharao, Cesar Augustus, Annunciacio,* and *Salutacio Elezabeth*—none (except, again, *Pharao*) contains any of the Wakefield Master's most characteristic devices. The Master or poets of his school seem to have revised much of the Towneley MS cycle, and as a rule those pageants which do not show clear signs of revision by the Wakefield Master have unmistakeable dramatic virtues of their own—for example, the Harrowing of Hell, the Resurrection, and the Ascension. Then why should a group of guildsmen who knew these more spectacular pageants, or an audience who had these pag-

65

eants for comparison, accept several hours of rather dull writing on Isaac, Jacob, the Prophets, and the rest?

The right answer may well be simply that the writers, guildsmen, and audiences were willing to shrug off a few bad pageants. Nevertheless, certain desperate defenses of these pageants can be offered. One is that these pageants involve audience emotions we have lost. Another is that, though dull as written texts, the pageants were interesting as spectacle, making use of theatrical machines and sets not recorded in the written text, and depending on acting styles about which we can only make guesses. A third explanation is that the number of guilds requiring pageants in fifteenth-century Wakefield put the Towneley MS poet or poets in an awkward position; they must provide pageants on minor events in the *Corpus Christi* scheme, yet they must somehow preserve the rhythm of "the play called Corpus Christi" as a whole.

Let us begin this chapter's speculations with a quotation from Professor O. B. Hardison, Jr.:

> Verisimilitude is a corollary of the shift from ritual to representation. Its manifestations include imitative costumes and stage props, correlation of action with dialogue, use of popular lyric forms instead of liturgical antiphons and scriptural paraphrase, character consistency, anachronism, and elimination of ceremonial and symbolic elements [e.g., the thurible as a figure of Christ]. Strict verisimilitude is never achieved on the stage unless, perhaps, in the drama of the school of Ibsen. Needless to say, it is found only in tentative and irregular forms in medieval drama, and when conflicts develop, it takes a second place to fidelity to source.[3]

Professor Hardison's remarks are a valuable corrective to earlier scholars' too-facile talk of "secularization." The improvisation of medieval playwrights operated within strict limits. One could make up antics, literal or symbolic, for the shepherds watching on the night of the Nativity, but for the adoration itself one must stay close to tradition. So too in the Noah pageant one might improvise on Noah's wife, creating interesting drama, but God's instructions to Noah, however boring, must be reported. Where tradition was silent, the playwright might say what he pleased; but where scripture and well-known commentary tradition led, he must follow. This is the first limit placed on improvisation.

There is perhaps a second. The playwright asked to do pageants on

Isaac's blessing of Jacob, or Jacob's flight and return, found himself
in an awkward situation if he was concerned about the *Corpus Christi*
drama as a whole. As Professor Hardison makes clear in the epilogue
to *Christian Rite and Christian Drama,* the *Corpus Christi* drama is,
in general outline, a huge imitation of the church-year ritual drama
of the Mass. In Amalarius's *Eclogae de officio missae,* the *Lectio* and
intermediate texts are treated as Old and New Testament "prepara-
tions" for the advent of Christ.[4] The shift from reading to chant is
for Amalarius "an indication of the rising pitch of excitement."[5] This
short chapter is no place for detailed treatment of the parallel dramatic movement of the Mass and the Wakefield *Corpus Christi* play
as a whole, but this much is clear at a glance: the Old Testament
pageants and the New Testament Annunciation and Salutation pre-
pare for and build toward a dramatic climax, the Nativity, exactly as
Amalarius says the Mass does. In a mystery cycle already containing
highly wrought pageants on Cain and Abel, Noah, and Abraham,
some leveling off in the pageants preceding the Nativity pageant is
very nearly an aesthetic necessity.

Seen in the perspective of these two limiting factors, the *Isaac* fragment appears at least excusable. Nearly all of the pageant is lost,
though we can easily guess what it contained. In the thirty-five couplets extant we have only Isaac's blessing of Jacob, his discovery of
Jacob's trick, his feeble blessing of Esau, and the decision of Isaac
and Rebecca to send Jacob away to Leben where he will be safe from
Esau's wrath. For the little he presents, the playwright depends entirely on his source, not so much scripture itself as the tradition de-
scending from Augustine's brief commentary on the birthright story
(*City of God,* XVI, 37). The playwright quotes the scriptural dialogue
Augustine quotes and passes over all other things; with one exception,
he introduces no imagery not singled out by Augustine. Of the available typology, Jacob's prefiguration of Christ and Esau's identification
as figure of the "old" or carnal man, the poet makes virtually nothing.
The allegory is present in the *Isaac* for those who know it already, but
it is not underscored by exegetical jokes or symbolic spectacle. Isaac's
words to Esau are the sole exception to this. Giving the only blessing
he has left, he says,

> god gif the to thyn handband
> the dew of heuen & frute of land;
> Other then this can I not say.

> (33–35)

The dew of heaven commonly figures grace or Christ, and in the spiritual sense the fruit is also Christ.[6]

Though what we have of the pageant is not highly wrought, it could make effective theater: the spectacle of the blind old man, the two sons bringing food, one of them in grotesque disguise, then bestial Esau's wrath and Rebecca's grief and alarm. Spectacle may have been all the playwright felt he had room for. Nothing can be made of character consistency because tradition denies the playwright that freedom. After being tricked, Isaac moves, without visible discomfort, to acceptance of the trick and defense of Jacob. Augustine comments:

> Who would not rather have expected the curse of an angry man here, if these things had been done in an earthly manner, and not by inspiration from above? Of things done, yet done prophetically; on the earth, yet celestially; by men, yet divinely![7]

The only other freedom left to the playwright is the freedom to make his characters talk like real people, and this much he does. Note Esau's exclamation, "Alas! I may grete and sob!" and the exchange between Rebecca and Isaac, closing with Isaac's lines, "Yei, son, do as thi moder says; / Com kys vs both & weynd thi ways" (65–66).

The second pageant in the group, *Jacob,* is also dull reading but must have been good theater. Here as in the *Isaac* pageant, scripture and commentary tradition severely limited what the playwright might do. Jacob was a type of Christ; his seed prefigured the "new Israel"; his vision of heaven and his wrestling match were profound mysteries not to be toyed with.[8] And also, here as in the *Isaac* pageant, the rhythm of the whole may have tended to inhibit improvisation. And so, like the *Isaac* playwright, the *Jacob* playwright limits himself to reproduction, unembellished, of the traditional allegory, and to an approximation of realistic human speech. Except for Jacob's siring children by four different women, on which Augustine offers a few passing remarks, the whole of Augustine's comment on the story (the basis of later commentary tradition) is brought over into the play; indeed, the play leaps, with its technique of "sliding time," from one Augustinian point or key scripture to another. Old Isaac's emphasis, and now God's, on Jacob's seed is explained as follows by Augustine: ". . . the seed of Jacob is separated from Isaac's other seed which came through Esau. For when it is said, 'In Isaac shall thy seed be called' [Gen. xii. 12], by this seed is meant solely the city of God. . . ."[9]

Talk of Jacob's seed occurs in the play at, for instance, lines 17–26, 69–70. Jacob's act of pouring oil on the stone altar is prophetic, Augustine says, "For Jacob did not pour oil on the stone in an idolatrous way, as if making it a god; neither did he adore that stone, or sacrifice to it. But since the name of Christ comes from the chrism or anointing, something pertaining to the great mystery was certainly represented in this."[10] Something of this allegory is brought into the pageant in Jacob's promise that if he is brought home in peace (home to heaven?) he will hold to his holy church forever (47–56); note especially the iconographic touch in lines 55–56—"This stone I rayse in sygne to day / shall I hold holy kyrk for ay." There may be further allegorical underscoring by the poet—in, for instance, Esau's possible second-level allusion to the Gospel in "tell me now som good tythand" (128)—but it would be pointless to insist on this. The pageant is, throughout, mainly literal and scriptural; indeed, the only real suggestion here that the playwright is looking both to scripture and to commentary tradition is that his selection of details happens to coincide with the selection of the commentators going back to Augustine. What is more noticeable in the text is the poet's imitation, at certain points, of realistic speech. Notice, for instance, Jacbo's lines early in the play:

> lord of heuen, thou help me!
> ffor I haue maide me, in this strete,
> sore bonys & warkand feete.
>
> (6–8)

One may notice, too, that the playwright introduces line-breaking of the kind found in the Abraham play or the kind which the Wakefield reviser introduced into his *Pharao,* lines 355–59, altering the borrowed York text *The Departure of the Israelites from Egypt,* lines 344–48. At the end of the wrestling match God asks Jacob: "What is thy name, thou me tell?" and this broken-line exchange ensues:

> *Iacob.* Iacob.
> *Deus.*   nay, bot Israell;
>   syn thou to me sich strength may kythe,
>   to men of erth thou must by stythe.
> *Iacob.* What is thy name?
> *Deus.*   whi askis thou it?
>   "wonderfull," if thou wil wyt.

> *Iacob.* A, blys me, lord!
> *Deus.*   I shall the blys,
>   And be to the full propyce. . . .
>
>   (93–100)

As I began by saying, if the Jacob pageant is dull reading it was probably good spectacle. In all probability it was spectacle that saved a pageant—made it worthwhile to the producing guild and to the audience—when improvisation was ruled out.

It was once a commonplace that the mystery pageants are primitive art. Perhaps so in their earliest form, but surely they were not by the fifteenth century. What was possible then can be gleaned from descriptions of early masques, from consideration of what was possible on the fixed stages of France, from what is implied in stage directions within the pageants, and from various account books and inventories of the guilds which produced the cycles. The *Ludus Coventriae* has this direction: "here Christ enteryth in-to the hous with his disciplis and ete the paschal lomb and in the mene tyme the cownsel hous beforn-seyd xal sodeynly onclose schewyng the busy-chopys prestys and jewgys syttyng in here Astat lyche as it were A convocacyone." Again: "Here The Buschopys partyn in the place And eche of hem takyn here leve be contenawns resortyng eche man to his place with here meny to make redy to take cryst and than xal the place there cryst is in xal sodeynly vn-close rownd Abowtyn shewyng cryst syttyng at the table and his dyscypulys eche in ere degre. . . ."[11] If the plays were originally produced on crude and simple pageant wagons, we know they were not always so produced. The sixteenth-century *Inventory of yᵉ p'ticulars appartaynyng to yᵉ Company of yᵉ Grocers* (1565) shows that late pageant wagons were elaborate and expensive.[12] We have also evidence that fine costumes were used,[13] and at least indirect evidence that some pageant stages or carts were equipped with mechanical devices that may have rivaled those of France. Professor Swart's remarks on the subject are worth quoting:

> All the four extant cycles include an Ascension play: Chester and N-town have a stage-direction saying that Jesus ascends; in the Wakefield play Jesus calls upon the clouds to open, and in the York play He asks for a cloud to be sent down to Him. We may be sure that there was a cloud which envelouped Him and carried Him up to Heaven. The alternative is in-acceptable. Or can we really believe that, even in a play,

Jesus, about to ascend to Heaven, could ask His Father to
send down a cloud to Him, and no cloud comes?

In many places the stage-directions and the text leave us in
doubt, but as in modern times, the producer was presumably
at liberty to create effects. One wonders, to mention only one
instance, what happens to the gossips in the Chester Noah.
Noah's wife is with them until she is forced to enter the ark,
and then we hear of the gossips no more. They could hardly
just stand back: in the play they symbolize the sinful world
that is destroyed. Ought we not rather to assume a very impressive scene, with a veritable deluge pouring down upon
them, while they descend, drinking and singing, to their doom?
The drunken voices waver and fade, and then suddenly we
hear only the strong and pure notes of Noah and his family
singing "Save me, O God!" as the ark rises upon the waters.[14]

Materials demanding theatrical treatment come up so frequently in
the English cycles that one may at last feel compelled to assume a
technically sophisticated stage. In one pageant after another, in all
the English cycles, angelic messengers appear, and frequently mysterious events occur—for instance the bells ringing by themselves in
the *Purificacio* of the Towneley MS. Herod's power to frighten the
audience (in one cycle he "ragis in the pagond and in the strete also")[15]
must surely come from the fact that his on-stage murders are convincing and his costume, which we know to have been expensive, impressive. The late Towneley MS Crucifixion and, even more so, the
Harrowing of Hell, would be all but unplayable on a crude early stage.

The likelihood, then, is that what was most impressive in Wakefield
productions of the Jacob play, and in other plays like it, was its spectacle. What that may have been, even assuming a sophisticated stage,
is anybody's guess. The facts of the text are that God appears (with,
scripturally, a ladder of angels, unmentioned in our text), and Jacob
responds by building and anointing an altar; by the convention of
sliding time, Jacob next appears with Rachel, Leah, and his army, and
then, in another swift leap forward in time, is discovered wrestling
with an angel, or Deus; after this he divides his army, meets Esau,
whose men have their swords drawn to kill him (see lines 129 sq.),
and makes peace with him. Even if the text were richer than it is, the
bulk of the pageant would be spectacle.

The next pageant, the *Processus Prophetarum,* is the dullest and
probably the oldest in the group, written in the romance stanzas com-

mon among the oldest pageants and devoid of drama, consisting, instead, of set speeches. It affords no opportunity for spectacle except in costume, and we need say nothing of it, except that a lull here in the cycle as a whole does, perhaps, no great harm to the larger drama. Then comes *Pharao*.

The chief interest of the *Pharao* has been, for scholars, that it derives from the York Play XI, *Departure of the Israelites from Egypt*, and allows us to study what happens to pageants as they pass from cycle to cycle. Pollard gives in his introduction to the EETS *Towneley Plays* a collection of the textual facts with which such study must deal, and since his list is familiar and generally sound it need not be reproduced here.[16] At some points, however, his observations need further comment. He contrasts Wakefield and York parallel lines to make the point that in "numerous instances . . . the Towneley text exhibits an unmetrical corruption of the York," and points to the following:

> [A] That wold my fors down fell (T. 32)
>   That wolde aught fand owre forse to fell (Y. 28)
>
> [B] That shall euer last (T. 39)
>   They are like and they laste (Y. 34)
>
> [C] I shall sheld the from shame (T. 189)
>   I shall the saffe from synne and shame (Y. 176)
>
> [D] What, ragyd the dwyll of hell, alys you so to cry (T. 304)
>   What deuyll ayles you so to crye (Y. 291)

I am inclined to suspect the Wakefield Master's hand or influence in some of these corruptions. The Wakefield line in the example I have labeled A, above, cavalierly drops a beat; example D cavalierly adds a beat, and also adds colloquial rant; in example B the Wakefield line introduces allegorical possibilities. Only example B needs comment. In the York text one of Pharao's advisers tells him, speaking of the prolific Jews,

> They multyplye so faste,
> þat suthly we suppose
> They are like, and they last,
> Yowre lordshippe for to lose.

                                                              (32–35)

The Towneley MS parallel reads:

> Thay multyplye fulle fast,
> And sothly we suppose
> That shalle ever laste,
> Oure lordshyp for to lose.
>
> (Smith, 33–36; Pollard, 37–40)[17]

The York lines can only be read literally. In the Towneley MS lines a second, allegorical level is possible: "The Old Israel, which prefigures the New, multiplies fast, and that people (the prefigured New Israel) will last forever, displacing earthly lords." Compare the exegetical jokes in the Wakefield Noah play, "This gere may neuer fayll" (274) of the ark (= church), and "This will euer endure" (283), and so on. Metrical carelessness for colloquialism or allegorical implication—or for no reason at all—is not rare in the work of the Wakefield Master.

At some points the Wakefield reviser adds new material, "surplusage," as Pollard calls it, which destroys the original stanza form. For instance:

> Fulle low he shalle be thrawne
> That harkyns not my sawe,
> Hanged hy and drawne,
> Therfor no boste ye blaw.
>
> (Pollard, 13–16)

We recognize the intrusive lines, or anyway their general sense: they are brought forward from the Herod play later in the cycle (see *Magnus Herodes*, line 81 and also Herod's general threats, lines 82–108); and they also parallel the Pilate speeches introduced into older plays, perhaps borrowed from Herod, in the Wakefield revisions, in the first stanza of the *Conspiracio* (3–9) and in *Fflagellacio* (4 sq.); and they parallel, too, Satan's lines in *Extraccio* (142 sq.). Pharao's vow "Fulle low he shalle be thrawne" looks back to Lucifer's fall from heaven and forward to his fall from the tower of hell in *Extraccio*. Without the bullying threats added to the York source, no specific connection between Pharao and Herod, etc., exists in the plays; yet the connection is obviously appropriate and valuable. The intrusive lines introduce connections between pageants, tightening the allegorical plot of the *Corpus Christi* play as a whole. In other words, the satanic undercurrent introduced through the character Garcio in *Mactacio Abel* (another bullying threatener) surfaces for a moment in *Pharao,* again in *Herod,* climaxes in the satanism of Pilate (see chapter nine, below), and is finally reversed in the Harrowing of Hell.

If we ignore metrical or stanzaic differences and concern ourselves solely with what has been added by the Towneley MS poet, we discover that he revises in two main ways, both of which support Professor Hardison's principle of fidelity to source. 1) He reintroduces important scriptural passages missing in the York version—for instance, Moses' removal of his shoes before the burning bush and his declaration that this is holy ground. 2) He improvises on the character of Pharao, adding exegetical jokes, introducing broken-line dialogue, and so forth. An instance of broken-line dialogue is the shift from the regular York text,

> *i. Egip.* My lorde, grete pestelence
>   Is like ful lange to last.
> *Rex.* Owe! Come that in oure presence,
>   Than is oure pride al past.
>
> (Y. 344–48)

to the Towneley version's—

> *Primus Miles.* A, my lord!
> *Pharao.*   hagh!
> *ijus Miles.* Grete pestilence is comyn;
>   It is like ful long to last.
> *Pharao.* In the dwilys name!
>   Then is oure pride ouer past.
>
> (T. 355–59)

At various points in the pageant, the playwright suggests allegorical extension of the literal situation. A soldier tells Pharao, "A, lord, alas, for doyll we dy! / we dar look oute at no dowre," and Pharao answers, "What, ragyd the dwyll of hell, alys you so to cry?" (302–4). Pharao's hypermetrical exclamation implies comparison of Moses' threat to Pharao's castle and Christ's threat to Satan's stronghold in the Harrowing play (cf. *Extraccio Animarum,* 116 ff).

What all this suggests is that the Wakefield revision of the York *Departure of the Israelites* play was made by the same principles as

the Wakefield revision of the York Cain play in *Mactacio Abel* (or
some related source): the reviser added allegorizing touches, intensi-
fied language here and there, and introduced material which con-
nected *Pharao* to other pageants in the cycle. He "secularizes" the
pageant somewhat further in his handling of language but drops no
scripture—in fact, he reintroduces passages dropped in the source.
If we assume a technically sophisticated stage and props—among
them a stick that can turn into a snake—we can guess that the
Pharao play may have been one of the more sensational of the
pageants.

The three pageants which follow, *Cesar Augustus,* the *Annunciacio,*
and the *Salutacio Elezabeth,* are all old, by Pollard's stanza test. Except that he is less interesting, one of the stock tyrants of the pageants, Cesar is like Pharao, a bullying threatener and, as usual in
the cycles, a worshiper of Mahowne. Like all the stock figures of
pride, he speaks lines more appropriate to God:

> I am lord and syr ouer all,
> All bowys to me, both grete and small,
> As lord of euery land;
>
> (19–21)

and so on. Nothing is done with all this (compare the puns and
comic exaggerations in the speeches of Herod later). Since scripture
and tradition do not limit the playwright in his treatment of Cesar,
why is the character not heightened by improvisation? Again, we
can only guess. To elaborate his tyranny would be to create simply
one more Herod-Pilate figure, detracting from the overall rising of
emotion in the "anticipatory" phase of the cycle as a whole. To
leave the pageant as it stands, on the other hand, is to restate in the
era approaching Christ's birth the cycle's important theme of the
pride and delusion of mortal kings:

> Commaunde the folk holly ichon,
> Ryche ne poore forgett thou none,
> To hold holly on me,
> And lowtt me as thare lord alone;
> And who wyll not thay shall be slone,
> This brand thare bayll shal be.
>
> (221–16)

The pageant gives no apparent opportunity for splendid theatrical effects; it is, as Pollard says of another pageant, more nearly a narrative poem than a drama.

Of the Annunciation pageant, Pollard has said all that need be said, I think; that of the simply devotional pageants it is the finest. The *Salutacio Elezabeth* has a similar tenderness and has one delightful early example of improvisation, the chatter of Mary and Elizabeth asking, as women have been doing since time began, about friends and relations. Their womanish talk shifts to babies, and then they tell each other the mysteries they know. The pageant ends, chatty again:

> ffarewell now, thou frely foode!
> I pray the be of comforth goode,
>   ffor thou art full of grace;
> Grete well all oure kyn of bloode;
> That lord, that the with grace infude,
>   he saue all in this place.

> (85–87)

The trouble with calling the older strata of pageants insipid is that even when they are, they are insipid by rules different from those applicable to modern drama. To judge the pageants well, we must visualize them in production, recognize their place in the *Corpus Christi* drama as a whole, and remember the extent to which our emotional response to the religious mysteries—the heart of these pageants—has changed since the Reformation. We must keep in mind George Raleigh Coffman's observation forty years ago: "They were intended to be presented. They were presented. They were popular."[18] Where innovations occur in the so-called process of secularization, there were reasons for these innovations, whether they be found in comic pageants like the Noah play or devotional pageants like the *Salutacio Elezabeth;* and where men who know how to improvise fail to do so, there may be reasons for that, too.

SIX

Light Dawns on Clowns:
Prima Pastorum

It is sometimes asked, "Why did Wakefield need two shepherds' pageants?" Since both are written in the nine-line stanza and the language of the Wakefield Master, and since, in both pageants, the stanzas operate from beginning to end, one must go on to ask, "Why did the Wakefield Master need to compose, himself, two separate shepherds' pageants?" The answer is virtually implied by the question. The first pageant gave him the idea for the second, an idea he liked so well he decided to use it. Why, then, did he not throw away the first, less effective pageant? Perhaps, though the first pageant is inferior to the second, it may have been viewed as no mean piece of work, a thing worth saving, perhaps even worth presenting from time to time.

The *Prima Pastorum* is a more interesting pageant than one would guess from the little critical attention it has received.[1] Much of what happens in *Secunda Pastorum* is dramatization in new form of ideas worked out in this earlier pageant. In both, life here on earth is parodic of life as it ought to be—that is, life in the New Jerusalem. In both pageants the three shepherds, in their weakness and limitation, dramatize the world's need for the incarnation of the tripartite God. And in both pageants the thematic focus is on appearance and reality or, in medieval terms, limited (carnal) vision and spiritual vision.

The fundamental comic conception behind the first shepherds' pageant is the contrast between the New Jerusalem and the Old, that is, between spirit and body, heaven and earth.[2] One kingdom is dignified and noble, the other farcical. The shepherds—Gyb, John Horn, and Slawpase (loosely, "Slowpoke")—are an early version of, say, the Marx brothers or the funnier of Beckett's tramps. They are, in effect, clowns (in the modern sense): Gyb a sad clown who wrings his fingers and bemoans his lot, John Horn a fierce clown—equivalent of the modern red-wigged bully of the circus—and Slawpase an equivalent of the modern bespectacled idiot savant. Jack Garcio, the servant, would be, in this analogy, equivalent to the circus ringmaster who can only rail or sigh at the lunacy of the clowns. As man is a fallen image of God, so the three foolish shepherds are a comic burlesque of infinite Goodness, Power, and Wisdom—the triune God who comes into the world at the end of the pageant, transforming life. The opening of the pageant focuses on the comically miserable condition of the shepherds and on their blindness; the progress of the pageant, beginning with Jack Garcio's remarks, dramatizes the traditional advent theme, the coming of light.[3]

Gyb's lament in his opening soliloquy is entirely concerned with man's misery—and especially his own—here in the realm of Fortune. The dead are lucky, he says, because their troubles are behind them. Here among the living

> . . . is mekyll vnceyll, and long has it last:
> Now in hart, now in heyll, now in weytt, now in blast;
> Now in care,
> Now in comforth agane;
> Now in fayre, now in rane;
> Now in hart full fane,
> And after full sare.
>
> (3–9)

He laments the senseless flip-flop of Fortune for another stanza, then states his own plight: his sheep are all dead, murdered by "the rott" —plague. His decision, which comes in the next two stanzas, is to forsake the farm (29) and, though he has nothing to bet, go to the fair (Vanity Fair is perhaps the implication) and try his luck with dice, or, as he says, "cast the warld in seuen" (38). The desperation of the plan is of course comically absurd. Since he is "With purs penneles" (33) and thus has nothing to bet, he is laying everything on chance—Fortune. The first throw had better be a lucky one, or instead of buying himself sheep, as he says he will do, he will get himself a drubbing. But Gyb has no choice, as far as he can see.

Looking no higher than this world, Fortune's realm—that is, failing to look beyond Fortune to controlling Providence—he sets his hopes on a thing not to be trusted. Gyb's own words reveal the mistake: "Now if hap will grynde, God from his heuen / Send grace!" (40–41) but Gyb misses the implications of his own flip exclamation. He means merely something like "Dear God give me luck!" (Compare Cain's exclamation, in *Mactacio Abel*, "bi hym that me dere boght, / I traw that he will leyn me noght" (114–15), where, as here, the exclamation, if taken seriously, comments on the character's mistake.)

Gyb's problem, at the beginning of the pageant, is physical want, province of the Fortune-starved concupiscent soul; his only hope, invisible before the Incarnation, is one aspect of the Trinity, God's Goodness (associated with the Holy Ghost).

The second shepherd's problem is fear. Jack Horn, though he later proves a bully himself, bemoans in his opening soliloquy the miseries which come

> From all myschefys,
> From robers and thefys,
> From those mens grefys
> That oft ar agans vs.

> (51–54)

He expands on this at length, talking of "bosters and bragers . . . / That with thare long dagers does mekyll wo," talking of "byll-hagers," "wryers and wragers," and so on (55sq.). He, too, in his sorry plight, has no hope but God, to whom he prays: "Help that thay were broght to a better way / For thare sawlys" (76–77), a comic prayer insofar as Horn's real concern is not the souls of evil-doers but his own physical welfare. Horn's problem, then, lies in the province of the irascible soul, insufficient in man, and appeals to a second aspect of the Trinity, God's Power.

As he is piously closing his soliloquy, Horn notices Gyb, the first shepherd, and calls to him. The exchange which follows suggests that Gyb is afraid of Horn, though not so frightened that he is willing to give way to him. "How, Gyb, goode morne!" John Horn calls out. "Wheder goys thou? / Thou goys ouer the corne! Gyb, I say, how!" Gyb, apparently sneaking away through the grain, feigns surprise (compare the language of Mak's feigned surprise when, after various tricks, he finally recognizes his old friends the three shep-herds—*Secunda Pastorum*, 219–20). "Who is that?" Gyb asks, and then, as if in amazement: "Iohn Horne, I make God avowe!" And he adds timidly, "I say not in skorne, Iohn, how farys thou?" (82–85). His phrase *I say not in skorne* makes sense, it seems to me, only as a comically desperate attempt not to offend an easily offended man.

What follows next is interesting, a typical Wakefield Master trick:

> *2 Pastor.* Hay, ha!
>   Ar ye in this towne?
> *1 Pastor.* Yey, by my crowne!
> *2 Pastor.* I thoght by youre gowne
>   This was youre aray.
>
> (86–90)

On the surface the exchange seems buffoonery. Horn's "ar ye in this towne?" is comparable to Mak's comically disingenuous greeting to the shepherds (in *Secunda Pastorum*) who have come to search his house: "Bot ar ye in this towne to-day?" (*SP*, 492). Gyb's emphatic "Yey, by my crowne!" is false heartiness. And Horn's response (absurd because they are not in town but in a field, and probably dressed not for town but for farming) is the comedy of inappropriateness. But the exchange operates on a second level. For an audience used to watching for exegetical jokes from the Wakefield Master— the comic Christology of Noah's wife, the eschatological double entendres of Cain ("Into som hole fayn wold I crepe" [*MA*, 337]; and compare the exegetical joking in *Secunda Pastorum*)—the exegetical overtones of this clownish nonsense should be obvious. Look at the rhymes: *towne, crowne, gowne, aray.* The lines comically contrast the sorry town of the play—the Old Jerusalem—with the new city announced by the nativity, where men will have crowns (not just pates), and where their dirty robes will be washed,[4] giving them nobler aray. Gyb's next line, too, has traditional overtones: "I am euer elyke, wote I neuer what it gars" (91). Compare Chaucer's pattern of verbal repetition on "ever yliche" in the *Book of the Duchess*, where the phrase describes three conditions, unchanging torment in hell, unrelieved despair on earth, and unchanging joy in heaven;[5] and compare the *Owl and the Nightingale*, lines 355–58.

The two clowns console each other, swapping comically inappropriate saws, some of them having exegetical overtones, and then Gyb lets it slip out that he means to buy sheep. John Horn, guarding his property rights against sheep that do not exist, and Gyb, jealously driving the nonexistent sheep, struggle to a comic impasse, from which Slawpase, an idiot who with comic arrogance believes himself wiser than his friends, labors to free them. To show them how once one wastes one's wits one cannot get them back, Slawpase dumps out his own sack of meal and challenges his two friends to put the grist back in the sack.

Slawpase is of course comically associated with intellect, or the rational soul. Whereas Gyb's problem has to do with concupiscence and can be solved only by divine Goodness, and whereas Horn's problem has to do with irascibility (the bullies he fears and represents) and can be solved only by God's ruling Power, Slawpase's problem is severely limited rationality and can be solved only by the Trinity's third member, Wisdom.

At this point Jack Garcio enters, servant of the three shepherds and, on the level of allegory, messenger of light. He scoffs at the shepherds—"foles all sam!" (179) and tells them,

> Wo is hir that yow bare! Youre syre and youre dam,
> Had she broght furth an hare, a shepe, or a lam,
> Had bene well.
>
> (181–83)

The lines seem to set up a comic contrast between the mother (or mothers) of the shepherds and the lady "blessed among women." And Garcio's reference to "an hare, a shepe, or a lam" seems a veiled allusion to the Lamb whose nativity is presented at the end of the play. The shepherds ask how their sheep are doing, and Garcio answers with the mysterious line, "Thay ar gryssed [grassed] to the kne" (189). Professor Cawley's note on the line is surely right: ". . . a symbol of midwinter fertility, a parallel in the world of nature to the miraculous birth of Christ. . . ."[6] Garcio seems to be saying that things are far better than the shepherds imagine, and if they will open their eyes they will see that this is so: "If ye *will* ye may se; youre bestes ye ken" (190; my italics). The line may possibly have a double sense: "You know your beasts" and "You know you are beasts," the second sense jokingly pointing out the carnality of the shepherds. In any case, the shepherds are cheered by Garcio's news, and they have a feast which parodies both the fine Christmas feasts of aristocrats in medieval England and the feast of the Eucharist. Exegetical jokes make the latter meaning clear. For instance, the third shepherd says,

I am worthy the wyne, me thynk it good skyll.
My serusyse I tyne; I fare full yll
At youre mangere.

(199–201)

In its richly elaborated detail—a sauced cow's foot, the leg of a
sow, a rotten ewe, and so on—the feast is of course insistently physical, not spiritual, "Good mete for a gloton" indeed (see line 222).
And the exegetical jokes throughout heighten the physicality of the
parodic celestial banquet.

> *3 Pastor.* . . .
> This is a restorité
> To make a good appeté.
> *1 Pastor.* Yee speke all by clergé,
> I here by youre clause.

(238–41)

Or compare the first shepherd's exclamation,

> A, so!
> This is *boyte of oure bayll,*
> Good holsom ayll.

(246–48; my italics)

Throughout all this, the shepherds alternate, with comic sudden-
ness, between good fellowship and brawling. For instance, when the
third shepherd empties the winecup, the first cries in outrage, looking into the cup, "Now, as euer haue I blys, to the bothom it is sonken"
(261), but when the second shepherd finds that there is still a full
bottle, the third shepherd makes peace with the first shepherd: "By
my thryft, we mus kys!" (263). And again, when the bottle is empty,
and the third shepherd calls the others knaves, the first and second
shepherds make peace:

> *1 Pastor.* Nay, we knaues all; thus thynk me best,
> So, syr, shuld ye call.
> *2 Pastor.*   Furth let it rest;
> We will not brall.

(278–80)

The scene ends with an act of not altogether admirable charity by the shepherds. Since they have used up the wine, without which the rotten food cannot be swallowed, they decide to give the food away.

> *3 Pastor.* Syrs, herys!
> For oure saules lett vs do
> Poore men gyf it to.
> *1 Pastor.* Geder vp, lo, lo,
> Ye hungre begers, frerys!
>
> (282–86)

Now the shepherds sleep and an angel brings the tidings dimly adumbrated in Garcio's speech. The shepherds awaken and talk, in comically colloquial language, of the angel's song. (The humor here is used again in *Secunda Pastorum*.) They recall, after a time, the words of the prophets, Lactantius's sybils, and Vergil, and they become convinced intellectually—if one can speak of intellect in connection with these three—of what the angel told them. Full of joy, they render (with various scoffing jokes at Slawpase, who thinks he remembers the angel's whole song, exactly like Coll in *Secunda Pastorum*) a grisly parody of the angelic music, then eagerly set out for Bethlehem. They are by now aware themselves that they are approaching full vision:

> *1 Pastor.* Wold God that we myght this yong bab see!
> *2 Pastor.* Many prophetys that syght desyryd veralee,
> To haue seen that bright.
> *3 Pastor.*   And God so hee
> Wold shew vs that wyght, we myght say, perdé,
> We had sene
> That many sant desyryd,
> With prophetys inspyryd;
> If thay hum requyryd,
> Yit closyd ar thare eene.
>
> (440–48)

And light does indeed come, first in the sky, imagistically, then in the manger, as the light of full knowledge. Whereas it was dark when they began the trip to Bethlehem (the first shepherd comments

at the start of the journey, "No lyght mase the mone" [434], the
sky brightens as they progress:

> *1 Pastor.* Abyde, syrs, a space. Lo, yonder, lo! It commys on
> a rase, yond sterne vs to.
> *2 Pastor.* It is a grete blase! Oure gate let vs go. Here he is!
>
> (450–53)

They see the child, give him their gifts, and leave as new men. The
parodic "restorité" of the rotten food in their earlier feast (238) has
given way now to true spiritual restoration: "We mon all be re-
storde—God graunt it be so!" (496); and after their earlier brawling
in darkness they can now say—the final line o the pageant—"Syng
we in syght."

SEVEN

Structure and Tone
in the *Secunda Pastorum*

The *Secunda Pastorum* is in a sense a revision of the *Prima Pastorum*. The three clowns of the earlier pageant are replaced by three realistic characters—but the function of the new characters remains much the same. And the blindness and illusion themes of the *Prima Pastorum* are again present in *Secunda Pastorum,* transformed to drama in the Mak episode. As art, of course, the revision leaves the rough draft far behind.

The *Secunda Pastorum*[1] is in a sense an exploration of the Christian significance of the number three: the pageant focuses on three shepherds; it begins with three soliloquies which open the first of three distinct movements; it treats three motifs appropriate to the Nativity story—law, charity, and wonder—and associates these motifs with parts of the Holy Trinity; it closes with three adorations of the Christ child and the giving of three symbolic gifts. The threes are by no means simply graceful embellishment. They are the heart of the matter.

Most productions of the pageant, whether in Middle English or in modern English, are theatrically effective in that they preserve the comic warmth and the spectacle which have made this the most enduring of medieval mysteries, but I know of no modern production which gives one a sense of the playwright's control of form. It can probably be taken for granted that modern audiences are less quick to perceive Christian number symbolism than was the poet's immediate audience; nevertheless, careful direction of the pageant, based on a careful reading of the text, ought to preserve and con-

vey the poet's artistic intention. Rather than treating the music in
the pageant as simple stage business or brief transitional material,
the director might emphasize the three-part structure of the pageant
by giving full and serious treatment to the music which separates
the parts, that is, the shepherds' descant at the end of the first
movement, the angel's song at the end of the second, and the shepherds' song at the end of the third. Rather than treating the shepherds simply as three country fellows, the director might individual-
ize their very different roles to emphasize the significance of each.
And rather than striving to achieve a fluid progression of the opening soliloquies or a dramatic interaction of the shepherds in their
first scene, the director might emphasize the separate importance of
each soliloquy by isolating characters on stage, or in a strictly modern production by spotlighting each of the three speakers in turn
while he is delivering his soliloquy. The *Secunda Pastorum* is not,
after all, modern: for all its comic realism, the pageant has the
formal balance of a medieval masque or, better, of certain types of
medieval religious verse ultimately derived, like the pageants, from
liturgy.

The theme of the pageant is the meaning of the Nativity, and
to develop his theme the poet explores three motifs appropriate to
the Christmas story. The first motif, set up in the opening soliloquy
of Coll, is lordship, or law, specifically the false lordship and sub-
version of law found in these "gentlery-men," who contrast with the
true lord, Christ. The second motif, set up in the opening soliloquy
of Gyb, is charitable love, perverted in the shrewish dominance of
women over men, the unseemly "headship" of imperfect women,
who contrast with the submissive and charitable Virgin.[2] Both of
the first two soliloquies are built upon the medieval commonplace
of relationship between order in human society and the total order
of the cosmos: each speaker moves from talk of the unnatural weather
to talk of another kind of disorder. The third motif, set up in Daw's
soliloquy, follows naturally: it is the motif of the wonderful, in the
old sense.[3] This motif interprets the cosmic disorder and provides
dramatic preparation for the Nativity which will herald a new order.

All three soliloquies focus first on the unnaturally bad weather.
Coll speaks in his first stanza of "stormes and tempest, / Now in
the east, now in the west" (7); Gyb says in his first stanza:

> Lord, thyse weders ar spytus, and the wyndys full kene,
> And the frostys so hydus thay water myn eeyne—
> No ly.

Now in dry, now in wete,
Now in snaw, now in slete,
When my shone freys to my fete
It is not all esy.

(57–63)

Daw's soliloquy establishes the fact that these are no ordinary winter storms: "It is wars then it was," he says, and:

Was neuer syn Noe floode sich floodys seyn,
Wyndys and ranys so rude, and stormes so keyn—

(127–28)

Daw is reminded of the uncertainty of life on earth, a theme common in the lyrics of the day and always expressed in much the same language, whether the theme is found in a sophisticated poem like "Summer Sunday" or a lullai:

Ne tristou to this world, hit is thy ful vo,
The rich he makith pouer, the pore rich al so;
Hit turneth wo to well and ek wel to wo—
Ne trist no man to this world, whil hit turnith so.
Lollai, l[ollai], litil child, the fote is in the whele;
Thou nost whoder turne to wo other wele.[4]

Daw develops this same theme in language which at once calls up the *vanitas, vanitatum* tradition in popular poetry and the storm imagery presented earlier, for his expressions "euer in drede," "brekyll as glas," "slythys," and "wrythys" all function doubly:

Whoso couthe take hede and lett the warld pas,
It is euer in drede and brekyll as glas,
And slythys.
This warld fowre neuer so,
With meruels mo and mo—
Now in weyll, now in wo,
And all thyng wrythys.

(120–26)

Whereas Coll's soliloquy and Gyb's dramatize the world's crying need for the Nativity which will conclude the pageant, Daw's soliloquy also dramatizes the sure proximity of that Nativity. More specifically, Coll's soliloquy dramatizes man's need for Christ as lord of man, since true lordship is not to be found in the world; Gyb's dramatizes man's need for Christ as lover of humanity and for the Virgin, emblem of charity, since nowadays young men who go courting are likely to get a woman like Gyb's, "as sharp as thystyll, as rugh as a brere;" and Daw's soliloquy dramatizes the wonder of Nature-in-disorder, a condition which cries for correction through a greater wonder, the advent of Christ. These three motifs order the action moment by moment and also account for the three distinct movements in the play.

After the three soliloquies, the poet presents a brief struggle between, on one side, Coll and Gyb, the masters, and, on the other, Daw, the servant. Daw asks for supper, his masters tease him, and Daw berates masters in language which recalls Coll's complaint against "gentlery-men" earlier. Daw says:

> Sich seruandys as I, that swettys and swynkys,
> Etys oure brede full dry, and that me forthynkys.
> We ar oft weytt and wery when master-men wynkys;
> Yit commys full lately both dyners and drynkys.
> Bot nately
> Both oure dame and oure syre,
> When we haue ryn in the myre,
> Thay can nyp at oure hyre,
> And pay vs full lately.
>
> (154–62)

Then Daw asserts that since masters will not treat servants fairly, he will repay his masters with bad work; and when Gyb asks where the sheep are pastured, Daw says he left them, early this morning, to wander "in the corne." Order—essentially the feudal order, a reflection of the order of the cosmos—seems undone. But in fact all three shepherds are, in their rough, country fashion, joking. Only a moment ago Daw was considering giving the sheep a turn, so it would seem they have not been left wandering since morning, "in the corne."[5] And now the shepherds, actually at one, sing together to warm themselves.[6]

Here ends what I call the first movement of the pageant—for the pageant breaks not into two parts, as some readers have argued, but into three. The opening soliloquies are impressive and for the most part serious poetry, and though the teasing which follows the solilo-

quies provides a transition toward the comic second movement involving Mak and Gill, the first movement concludes with some of
the seriousness of its beginning. The second movement ends with the
blanket-toss, and the third ends the pageant. Music signals the divi-
sions: the shepherds sing as the second movement opens; an angel
sings as the third movement opens (after a one-stanza transition from
the blanket-toss); and the shepherds sing again as the pageant ends.
Each of these movements emphasizes one of the motifs set up in
the three soliloquies without discarding the other motifs. The first
movement focuses on the master-servant relationship, mainly, the
second focuses on the idea of love (on one hand, the conflicts of a
married couple, Mak and Gill, on the other hand, the brotherly love
of shepherds who want no enemies, love children, and prefer to let
thieves off lightly); and the third movement focuses on the Nativity
mystery.

If the pageant is viewed in this way, Mak's entrance, initiating
what I have called the second movement, does not in the least in-
terrupt the development of the poet's theme. Mak speaks first of how
God has mistreated him ("thi will, Lorde, of me tharnys") by giving
him too many children. But Mak's complaint against his Lord is not
quite honest, as he hints in his aside (line 196): thanks to his trade,
Mak fares better than he would want the shepherds to know. The
shepherds snatch Mak's cloak, presumably to look for loot under-
neath it or in the sleeves, as J. H. Smith has suggested,[7] and Mak's
reaction further develops the lordship motif—indignantly (and
falsely) Mak tells the shepherds that he is a yeoman of the king.
The shepherds scoff, and the conversation turns to a more central
concern in this movement, Mak's marital problems. Mak's Gill, it
seems, is a living emblem of all Gyb complained against earlier.
When the shepherds fall asleep, Mak's activities relate to the third
motif: wonder is perverted in Mak's charm against creatures of the
night. Since Mak is a night creature himself, a comic devil figure,
he commends himself not to God but to *Poncio pilato,* who in this
Corpus Christi cycle becomes Satan's earthly vicegerent (see chapter
nine). And wonder is again perverted in Mak's use of the magic
circle.

In the next scene, between Mak and Gill, the poet focuses on the
improper and uncharitable relationship of Mak and his wife. When
Mak comes, Gill will not open the door for him. The reason she
gives is that she is working and cannot be interrupted, and she makes
much of the work of women. But the truth is that Gill is doing

one of the only two things she is good at (cf. line 237), getting drunk.
When Gill finally does let him come in, Mak says:

> Do way!
> I am worthy my mete,
> For in a strate can I gett
> More than thay that swynke and swette
> All the long day.
>
> Thus it fell to my lott, Gyll; I had sich grace!
>
> (309–13)

In the fourth and fifth lines quoted here, Mak is alluding to the
parable of the vineyard (Matthew 20:12), a parable commonly treated
by the schoolmen as the scriptural comment on salvation by grace
as opposed to salvation by works. If Gill perverts works, Mak perverts grace; both therefore pervert cosmic order, for works are the
lawful duty of the vassal and grace is the gift to the vassal from the
lord.[8] Not, of course, that we take all this very seriously. The twist-
ing of scripture and, above all, the visual joke—the Lamb won by
theft—rule out any hint of somber theology.

The improper nature of the Mak-Gill relationship is established
not only by Gill's refusal to obey her husband but also by her thinking for him. The poet's immediate audience must have caught at
once the significance of the lines,

> This is good gyse and a far-cast;
> Yit a womman avyse helpys at the last.
>
> (341–42)

The danger of taking a woman's advice was firmly rooted in biblical
tradition and was universally acknowledged, though sometimes half-
jokingly. The stock idea appears again and again in Chaucer, is
central to Sir Gawain's fall (at least from Gawain's point of view),
provides humor in numerous lyrics, and receives serious treatment
from church writers. And the basis of Gill's mistake, it should be
noticed, is the basis of Eve's—pride. (Here again, of course, the contrast with the Virgin is important.) Gill reminds Mak repeatedly
that only she could have thought of such a trick, and later, when
the shepherds are about to arrive, Gill regrets that the trick is not
even bolder: "If it were a gretter slyght, yet couthe I help tyll"
(433).

Both as outlaws and as a married couple whose proper male and female roles are reversed, Mak and Gill in a sense epitomize that fall from order which characterizes this world. Not everyone must perforce be a thief and not every man must perforce be a henpecked husband, but thieves and henpecked husbands are more common in this world, the poet suggests throughout, than honest men and husbands who rule. Mak and Gill thus present an exaggeration of the common human situation; their story serves as a natural foil for the Bethlehem story.

The scene in which the shepherds search for the sheep and then adore the "child" serves chiefly as a comic contrast to the shepherds' adoration of the Christ child. But the comic scene is not gratuitous, nor is it merely symbolic. When the shepherds believe they have accused Mak falsely, they humbly and charitably ask that there be harmony between Mak and themselves. The proud and uncharitable Mak will have none of it. And when the shepherds realize that they have given the child no presents, they return. Thus it is the shepherds' charity and lack of overweening pride that uncovers the trick, and the same qualities afterward recommend them as servants of the Christ child. The one speech the poet gives to the Virgin sums up those qualities. She reveals her own submissiveness to the will of God and Christ, charitably promises to beg her son to preserve the shepherds from harm, and tells the shepherds to bear in mind what they have seen today:

> The fader of heuen, God omnypotent,
> That sett all on seuen, his son has he sent.
> My name couth he neuen, and lygth or he went.
> I conceyuyd hym full euen thrugh myght, as he ment;
> And now is he borne.
> He kepe you fro wo!
> I shall pray hym so.
> Tell furth as ye go,
> And myn on this morne.
>
> (737–45)

The shepherds are filled with grace, and the end of the pageant, like the end of the first movement, is a song.

It should be evident that the *Secunda Pastorum*, sometimes described as disjointed, has surprising orderliness. The three motifs set up in the opening soliloquies appear in the same order in the three movements of the play; when shifts from one motif to another appear within individual scenes, they appear in order (for instance, when Mak finds the shepherds, at the beginning of the second movement, the poet focuses first on Mak as false vassal, then on Mak as husband, then on Mak as warlock). Moreover, once all three shepherds are on stage, the three alternate with considerable regularity throughout the pageant,[9] and the pattern of alternating speeches in the first and third movements corresponds both to the order of the soliloquies and to the order in which the shepherds adore the Christ child.

The structural coherence of the *Secunda Pastorum* is reinforced by a coherence of tone based on consistent and symbolic characterization of the three shepherds. Through his characteristic behavior, each shepherd comes to be associated with the motif introduced in his opening soliloquy; and through his thematic function, that is, through his association with lordship or charity or wonder, each of the three shepherds calls to mind a specific aspect of the Trinity. Coll comes to be related to Wisdom, Gyb to Love, Daw to Power. This is not to say that Coll, Gyb, and Daw *represent* aspects of the Trinity but only that each shepherd has a characteristic concern. Coll, though by no means an allegorical figure of Divine Law, is characterized as a man concerned with the meaning and order of things; Gyb, who genially teases his friends and thus would cut a poor figure as Divine Love, is characterized as an essentially friendly, gentle man who wants harmony with others; and Daw, whose passion is that of a child and servant—passion unchecked by reason—summons to mind, by contrast, true and meaningful power.[10]

The first shepherd, Coll, is old; he is a man who has suffered and thought and learned a homely dignity. As the play opens, Coll stands alone. He knows the difference between true nobility and your gentlerymen, but he knows, too, the futility of railing. He has that ideal quality of both lords and vassals in the Christian feudal scheme, patience. (Cf. the medieval poem, *Patience,* or see Chaucer's *Franklin's Tale,* lines 761–75.) When Daw tells him the sheep have been left in the corn (i.e., grain) where, as Daw says, "thay can not go wrong," Coll retorts with wry humor, "That is right, by the roode" —that is, I take it, grain is excellent food. (As far as I can see, this is the only clear sign in the pageant that Coll has a sense of humor.) But then, ending the teasing, Coll comments on the length of these winter nights and sensibly suggests that he and his fellows warm themselves by singing. When Mak plays his first trick, pretending to be a yeoman of the king, Coll responds directly: "Why make ye it so qwaynt? Mak, ye do wrang." It is Coll who asks about Mak's wife; Coll who insists, after the loss of the sheep, that Mak's guilt be proved ("Thou sklanders hym yll"); Coll who apologizes to Mak when the shepherds have found nothing in Mak's house; Coll who remembers that the child should be given some present; and Coll who argues for compassion, opposing Daw's facile righteousness. One's view of tone in the pageant, then, must take account of Coll's stablizing humanity.

Gyb, in his opening soliloquy, speaks of the woes of the married man. The tone of his speech is ambivalent, for while he mocks the bondage of marriage, he does so with such humor, and such obvious delight in sex, that one cannot tell whether or not he really does wish he had run till he had escaped marriage:

> Sely Copyle, oure hen, both to and fro
> She kakyls;
> Bot begyn she to crok,
> To groyne or to clok,
> Wo is him is oure cok,
> For he is in the shakyls.
>
> (67–72)

A similar ambivalence informs the lines which follow soon after as Gyb marvels at the thought that "Som men will have two wyfys and som men three / In store." But Gyb's playful ambivalence is not limited to his view of marriage. When he learns that Daw is coming, just before Daw's soliloquy, Gyb says gleefully, "He wyll make us both a ly / Bot if we be war." When Daw asks for food, Gyb teases him, pretending that rules which operate in a well-ordered household also operate in the fields:

> Though the shrew came late,
> Yit is he in state
> To dyne—if he had it.
>
> (151–53)

When Mak comes, Gyb teases him just as he teased Daw. Slyly, as though he personally would never entertain such suspicions, Gyb tells Mak,

Shrew, pepe!
Thus late as thou goys,
What wyll men suppos?
And thou has an yll noys
Of stelyng of shepe.

(221–25)

But in all Gyb's jibing there is a certain gentleness, the familiar
wish of the genial prankster that there be no hard feelings. When
Mak's house has yielded up no sheep, Gyb asks that Mak and the
shepherds part friends. When Coll asks, "Gef ye the chyld any
thyng?" Gyb responds, startled, "I trow not oone farthyng!" And
when Mak's secret is out, Gyb's response is not righteous indignation
but amused admiration for the ingenuity and daring of the trick.
If Coll brings to the action humanity and dignity, Gyb brings a
playful gentleness.

Daw is of course a child, and his emotions are the volatile emotions natural in a child. In his opening soliloquy he speaks ear-
nestly of marvels; to Gyb's teasing he responds with petulance; to
the disappearance of the sheep he responds with melodramatic accu-
sations. When Coll asks, "Gaf ye the chyld any thyng?" Daw rushes
back to make amends. When he meets Mak at the door—Mak whom
only a moment ago he treated rudely—Daw exclaims, "Mak, take
it to no grefe if I com to thi barne." His persistence in teasing for
a glimpse of the "child" and his double-functioning epithets ("that
lytyll day-starne") reveal his love of, even reverence toward, the newborn. But in his changeable way he is capable of outrage the next
instant, for he finds the trick not amusing but wicked:

Lett bren this bawde and bynd hir fast.
A fals skawde hang at the last;
So shall thou!

(595–97)

To view the three shepherds in this way is to see both the complexity and the coherence of tone in the pageant. Coll's opening
soliloquy is a solemn and poetically effective treatment of the ordinary human condition. Gyb's opening speech on disorder in the
world picks up Coll's tone, then shifts to a more playful tone but
one not entirely playful. Daw's soliloquy, like Gyb's, begins solemnly
and grows lighter at the close (when he realizes that Coll and Gyb

are spying). The exchange between Daw and Gyb is light but brief, giving way to the three-part song which has, at least, serious overtones: the shepherds have patched up their trifling differences. The Mak-Gill episode is hilarious but by no means merely farcical, for Coll lends moral dignity, Gyb lends gentleness, Daw brings impulsive changes. Moreover, Mak, however charming and harmless in the pageant, does introduce, in his character as false God or devil, darker possibilities—the war of Christ and Satan. Even when the song of the angel comes, the shift in tone is not complete. Gyb is impressed by the beauty of the angel's song; Coll more reflective, commenting that he can remember the song word for word; and even at a time as solemn as this, Gyb cannot resist ribbing the old man: "Let se how ye croyne. / Can ye bark at the mone?" Daw, the impulsive, objects to Gyb's profanation and cries out. "Hold youre tonges, have done!" The true Nativity follows, a scene which is moving not only because it contrasts with all that has gone before but also because it illuminates and fulfills all that has preceded it. Coll, associated with order, lordship, addresses the child as "Maker" and speaks of Christ's victory over the devil, then, with characteristic humanity, delights in the laughter of the child, whom he calls "my swetyng;" Gyb, associated with love, hence with a second aspect of the Trinity, addresses the child as "Savior," then, with characteristic playfulness, familiarly calls the child "lytyll tyne mop;" and Daw, associated with a third aspect of the Trinity, says to the child: "I pray the be nere when that I haue nede," then, with the same love of children he has shown before, calls the child "derlyng dere" and comments, "swete is thy chere!"

The gifts which are offered are also symbolic. Professor Cawley suggests in his notes to lines 718 and 722 that the bird and the ball are to be associated with, respectively, the Holy Ghost and the Father. Of the cherries he says, "This unseasonable gift, which is a traditional Christmas miracle, can be taken as a symbol of midwinter fertility, a parallel in the world of nature to the miraculous birth of Christ." The image, in other words, is emblematic.[11]

In presenting the *Secunda Pastorum*, the director's problem is to show the audience that, far from introducing original material into the Nativity story merely to entertain the crowd, merely to stretch out an otherwise brief story, or merely to give rein to his comic realism, the poet has used lifelike English shepherds to dramatize what was for him and for most of his contemporaries the meaning of Christmas and the truth about our human condition.

EIGHT

Christian Black Comedy:
The *Magnus Herodes*

The two pageants which immediately follow the *Secunda Pastorum* in the Towneley MS are both dull as literature (perhaps not as theater). The *Oblacio Magorum* has one interesting prosodic device in the opening stanzas, rhyme linking like that in *Pearl* or the lyric *Summer Sunday*. The first stanza ends "The lord am I" and the second begins, "Lord am I of every land;" the second stanza ends "Both man and wyfe," and the third begins "Man and wyfe . . ." and so on. But at the end of the sixth stanza the poet drops the device as too troublesome (unless the change marks, as I think it does, the poet's shift to a new source). In construction the *Oblacio* is loose, casual, merely serviceable: Herod rants about his power, then sends a messenger to learn of any citizens not loyal to Mahowne; the Magi talk of the star, meet the messenger, and go with him to Herod, who commands them to tell him whatever they may discover about the Christ child; warned by an angel, they disobey. Except for the endless speeches, the method is economical: the succession of scenes gets the job done, and no doubt costume, and perhaps other effects, made the play acceptable on stage. The writing, throughout, is not only long-winded but poetically flabby, frequently snatching at rhymes by poetic padding—for instance:

> yond starne betokyns, *well wote I,*
> The byrth of a prynce, syrs, *securly,*
> That shewys well the prophecy . . .

(199–201; my italics)

More important, however, the play is literal throughout. Like the Herod of the far more impressive *Magnus Herodes,* Herod in this play pretends to power like God's, saying things that would be more appropriate to God:

> Lord am I of euery land,
> Of towre and towne, of se and sand;
> Agans me dar noman stand,
>   That berys lyfe;
> All erthly thyng bowes to my hand,
>   Both man and wyfe.
>
> (10–15)

But the appropriateness is only general; Herod does not borrow specific phrases from God, as does the Herod of *Magnus Herodes.* Only once in the play does the poet use language which might have direct exegetical overtones. He says to his messenger when the boy returns, "where has þou bene so long fro me" (261), a phrase curious and suggestive not so much in its own right as because it recalls one of Noah's wife's many unwitting exegetical jokes (*Processus Noe,* 192). In the Noah the second-level possibility is reinforced by other jokes. Here the playwright seems unaware of the symbolic possibilities. He does not make Herod a consistent parody of God or the messenger a parody of God's emissary. The *Oblacio* throws light on the *Magnus Herodes,* then, not by what it does but by what it does not do. All indications are that the play is either borrowed by Wakefield and left unchanged or is, as Pollard believed, a play from the earliest of the three stages of composition to be found in the cycle, the stage which made use of a favorite meter "of the fourteenth-century romances which were already going out of fashion in Chaucer's day."[1]

Of the next play in the Towneley MS, the *Fugacio Iosep & Marie in Egiptum,* nothing need be said: it is, like the *Oblacio,* a simple piece probably written long before Wakefield could afford a cycle, then borrowed and produced unchanged except for the faults in meter and stanza form to be expected in pirated plays. In original production, somewhere other than Wakefield, the pageant must have been very simple indeed. We may suppose that in Wakefield, where sophisticated fifteenth-century wagons or stages were surely available, the angelic visitation may have been handsomely theatrical. Be that as it may, the *Fugacio* does have one important virtue if we view it in its context. It relieves the relatively dark tone of the *Oblacio* with its timorous and shining sweetness and provides a calm before the storm of the great black comedy *Magnus Herodes*.

In the Wakefield Master's Herod pageant, Herod is insistently allegorical. The comic premise of the pageant is the same as the premise discovered in, for instance, the *Prima Pastorum* and the *Mactacio Abel*: this world is a burlesque of heaven, and human beings parody Christ, either as types or as opposites—that is, devils. But whereas the comedy of earlier pageants was for the most part light-hearted (Noah, for example, is a likeable burlesque figure), the comedy here is—like the even grimmer comedy in such later plays as the *Coliphizacio*—black. The strategy by which the poet achieves his black humor is interesting. In the pageant's first movement, Herod, with all his grand pretensions, is ludicrous, provoking comfortable laughter at the disparity between what Herod imagines himself to be and what the Christian audience knows he really is. Then comes the bloody second movement—the soldiers' murder of children, the grief and impotent rage of the mothers, and the soldiers' scornful jokes. After this movement we return to Herod, who behaves exactly as before; but this time, if we laugh, the laughter has overtones of anger. Though Herod's pretensions are as absurd as ever, our memory of the second movement colors our response to the king's shenanigans.

The messenger who opens the Wakefield pageant establishes Herod's allegorical identity as parody of God. After giving Mahowne's blessing —Mahowne in this play is not only Herod's lord, as in the *Oblacio*, in the York Massacre of Innocents, etc., but also his cousin (54)—the messenger warns:

> Take tenderly intent
> What sondys ar sent,
> Els harmes shall ye hent . . .

> (6–8)

The lines ironically recall the very different "sondys" of the true God. (Cf. the well-known lyric beginning "The mirth of all this land / Maketh the good husband.") The messenger later makes the Herod-Christ parody more explicit:

> He is kyng of kyngys, kyndly I knowe,
> Chefe lord of lordyngys, chefe leder of law.
> Ther watys on his wyngys that bold bost wyll blaw;
> Grett dukys downe dyngys for his greatt aw
> And hym lowtys;

> (37–41)

Herod is "King of Kings" and has, at least metaphorically, "wings," like God. All the princes of this world bow to him. He rules all the earth, from "Tuskane and Turkey" even "vnto Kamptowne" (42–47). Borrowing the phrase with which medieval poets frequently suggest the inexpressible glory of God,[2] the messenger says,

> His renowne
> Can no tong tell,
> From heuen vnto hell;
>
> (50–52)

Calling Herod "worthyest of all barnes that ar borne," the messenger reminds the audience of another worthy newborn child, the Christ whom Herod burlesques. Herod's own speeches continue the parallel. He says, for instance:

> Peasse, both yong and old, at my bydyng, I red,
> For I haue all in wold: in me standys lyfe and dede.
>
> (91–92)

Spiritual life and death stand, of course, in Christ's hands. Herod's sway is more limited: "Who that is so bold, I brane hym thrugh the hede!" (93).

As a factitious kingdom of heaven, Herod's kingdom, the Old Jerusalem, is ridiculous. Since the text emphasizes, throughout, the lunatic pride, the pretentiousness and affectation of Herod and those around him, we may safely assume that spectacle ought to carry the same significance. Costume should be grotesquely ostentatious—spangled, bejewelled, etc. Since Herod's claim to omnipotence is nonsense, it seems likely that Herod ought not to be a great, burly fellow but ought to be instead a piping, squawking midget or a flaxen-haired, effeminate man—precisely a man like Chaucer's Absalon, in *The Miller's Tale,* who has played the part of Herod, Chaucer says. His knights should be great, hulking lumberjacks with the brains of subnormal monkeys, and they should be dressed—courageous battlers against babies—as if for war with dragons. Herod's wise men should be manifest fools; projectors. Such presentation of Herod and his court gives comic force to the messenger's remark, which he does not find in the least absurd, that

> For a boy that is borne herby
> Standys he [Herod] abast.
>
> (24–25)

It is Herod's terror over a rumor that points up the comedy of his
seeming puissance, power in fact based on nothing but his grisly dis-
position. The messenger warns of this grimness in Herod, and all the
court reacts to it.

> Begyn he to brall, many men cach skorne;
> Obey must we all, or else be ye lorne
> Att onys.
> Downe dyng of youre knees,
> All that hym seys;
> Dysplesyd he beys,
> And brykyn many bonys.
>
> (57–63)

Flimsy as he is, Herod wields a wicked scepter, banging the helmets of
his knights and howling his rage. He is forever talking of killing
people:

> Stynt, brodels, youre dyn—yei, euerychon!
> I red that ye harkyn to I be gone;
> For if I begyn, I breke ilka bone,
> And pull fro the skyn the carcas anone—
> Yei, perdé!
> Sesse all this wonder,
> And make vs no blonder,
> For I ryfe you in sonder,
> Be ye so hardy.
>
> (82–90)

And, again,

> Styr not bot ye haue lefe,
> For if ye do, I clefe
> You small as flesh to pott.
>
> (97–99)

Exegetical jokes provide the pageant's comment on Herod's real condition. Enraged at the news of Christ's birth, Herod rants:

> My myrthes ar turned to teyn, my mekenes into ire,
> And all for oone, I weyn, within I fare as fyre.
> May I se hym with eyn, I shall gyf hym his hyre; . . .
>
> (100–103)

Of Christ as Judge it may properly be said that his "meekness" at times turns to wrath; but Herod has no meekness, so far as one can see. In his phrase "I fare as fyre" Herod unwittingly alludes to his real destination. And when he says of Christ, "May I se hym with eyn, I shall gyf hym his hyre," he unwittingly echoes innumerable medieval religious poems which speak of seeing God with one's eyes (that is, face to face in heaven)—the alliterative *Purity,* for instance, where the phrase occurs repeatedly. "I shall gyf hym his hyre" is funny too, reversing the feudal relationship of God and man.

At the idea of Christ's someday becoming a greater king than himself, Herod is outraged. He rants on and on, affording the poet the opportunity to throw in numerous *doubles entendres;* for instance, "If I this crowne may bere, that boy shall by for all" (112). Christ will indeed "buy" for all. Later, giving the knights their orders—kill all boys under the age of two—Herod warns:

> Spare no kyns bloode,
> Lett all ryn on floode;
> If women wax woode,
> I warn you, syrs, to spede you.
>
> (312–15)

The image of blood running in a flood has exegetical overtones. Compare the *Pearl*-poet's lines:

> Innoghe þer wax out of þat welle,
> Blod and water of brode wounde . . .
>
> (*Pearl,* 649–50)

an image the *Pearl*-poet later develops as a flood from a ditch.[3] And part of the knights' response also has overtones:

> Hayll, heyndly!
> We shall for youre sake
> Make a dulfull lake.
>
> (320–22)

The doleful lake is the lake of damnation—the fiery lake of *St. Erkenwald,* the grim tarn of Chaucer's *Parlement of Foules,* in which fish gasp and die.

The scene which follows is shockingly brutal. If the Old Jerusalem is ludicrous, it is also monstrous. Irony grates throughout. Apparently

the power of the knights is as cheap—and as carnal—as that of Herod.
Approaching the women whose children they intend to kill, one of the
knights sends the others ahead, "while he himself hangs safely behind,"
Professor Cawley notes.[4] (Compare the soldiers' fear in the York play:
"As armes! for nowe is nede, / But yf we do yone dede, / Ther quenys
will quelle us here" [207–9].) To the first mother, the first knight says
with grotesque *gentilesse,* as if tipping his hat, partly as a sick kind of
joke but perhaps also seeking to evade her wrath by an apology,
"Dame, thynk it not yll, / Thy knafe if I kill" (330–31). The woman
cannot believe her ears and seems unable to decide whether the man
is joking or mad. She reacts as if to an obscene proposition—"What,
thefe, agans my wyll?" (332), tries to escape and, when the knight
catches her, reacts as if to sexual molesting: "Shall I chyde and make
here a nose?" (335). The knight says "I shall reyfe the thy pryde" (336),
meaning he will kill her son, her "pride," but using a phrase a man
might use to a wench putting on airs. Time will tell about that, she
answers, "kepe well thy nose" (337), a phrase which can be read as
sexual euphemism. She strikes him, and he responds with the word
implied throughout, "hoore" (340). He kills the child and all humor
drops momentarily from the play for the horror and anguish of the
mother's cry for vengeance. The second knight comments with black-
comic indifference, "Well done!" and turns to the second woman. He
scoffs at her cries for mercy, overcomes her physical resistance, and
kills the child. Like the first mother, she cries for vengeance. Then the
third knight takes his turn. He fights his woman as though she were
another knight—"Haue at the, say I!" (381)—striking her twice with
his sword (once in the groin). She too cries for the vengeance not visible
in the world before Christ's revelation: "of bales who may me borow?"
(389). Now the knights return to Herod, arguing, as they go, over who
shall be first to come before him—a parody of the dispute of Christ's
disciples.

   In Herod's hall the knights report on their work and ask for their
reward, physical parody of Christ's spiritual reward. Herod promises

>   castels and towers,
>   Both to you and to youres,
>   For now and euermore.

                                                              (448–50)

Then, as Christ calls men to himself, Herod tells the audience, "Draw
therfor nerehande" (462), and promises that—when he is ready—he

will reward them. "Wate when I com agayn," he says, "And then may ye craue" (467–68). At his next coming, parody of the Second Coming, the audience may ask what it wishes, he says; but the ironic overtone is "Then may ye go on craving." His entire final speech, like his opening speech, ironically echoes biblical language, grimly contrasting him with Christ. As Christ might say, but for a different reason, Herod says, "now my hart is at easse, / That I shed so mekyll blode" (469–70). As the ascending Christ might say, Herod says,

> So light is my saull
> That all of sugar is my gall!
> I may do what I shall,
> And bere vp my crowne.
>
> (474–77)

The number of the blessed in the New Jerusalem is the number of Herod's murders:

> A hundreth thowsand, I watt, and fourty ar slayn,
> And four thousand.
>
> (487–88)

He is, like Christ, an "example" for man (496), and when he returns, all things will stand revealed (507).

The Wakefield Herod pageant does not have in it much social criticism except for its general attack on all tyrants; it contrasts in this respect with other works entirely by the Wakefield Master. (Herod's bad French [lines 171, 273, and 512—cf., also, line 513] imitates a common affectation of pretentious medieval Englishmen, as does the French of Chaucer's Friar in the *Summoner's Tale* [*CT*, III, 1838].) What it does have in common with all the pageants by the same playwright is allegory, earth's burlesque of heaven, developed on a base of comic realism. It is partly this textural richness, partly the blackness of the comedy in Herod's final speech, without parallel in the Herod pageants of other cycles, which makes the Wakefield *Magnus Herodes* the best of the pageants on this subject. Within the larger scheme of the Wakefield *Corpus Christi* play, the Herod pageant reintroduces, in allegory, the satanic side of the conflict of Christ and Satan.

NINE

The Tragicomedy of Devil Worship: From the Conspiracy to the Play of the Talents

The two fragmentary pageants and the one complete pageant immediately following the *Magnus Herodes* in the Towneley MS—that is,
the pageant on the purification of Mary, the pageant on Christ
among the doctors (borrowed from York), and the pageant on John
the Baptist—provide another lull in the cycle, a lull which will be
followed by five monstrous, and often brilliant, pageants in succession: the pageants of the Conspiracy, the Buffeting, the Scourging,
the Crucifixion, and the Talents. All three of the pageants which
provide the lull are literal and static, hence only of slight interest
in themselves. But because of certain direct connections between the
Herod pageant which precedes them and the five-pageant series which
follows them, it will be useful to review them here. The whole movement, from Herod's pageant to the Crucifixion, is the usual third
or tragic movement of the overall "plot" in the *Corpus Christi* plays;
it should not surprise us unduly to find this movement structurally
integral in a sophisticated cycle.[1]

In the first of the three quiet pageants, old Symeon speaks nine
eight-line stanzas, mostly on the dreariness of old age, before two
angels come to answer his prayer. The remainder of the fragment—
only a few stanzas—is interesting for its lyricism and might be effective on an elaborate stage: bells ringing by themselves, Joseph and
Mary arriving at the temple with two doves. The doctors pageant
which follows is equally static and much more dull, the bulk of it
being devoted to Christ's flawless recitation of his catechism. The
pageant on John the Baptist is for us duller yet, because longer.

John talks to himself, then with Christ, then with angels, all on doctrine, and Christ gives him a lamb and explains the symbolism. John preaches, and the pageant ends. In meter and form it is the most perfect of the three quiet pageants and, by Pollard's generally accepted standard, may be considered an almost perfect MS preservation of a pageant from the earliest stage of composition within the Towneley MS. Its lack of revision, comic elaboration, or cutting for heightened drama is precisely what Hardison's principle on fidelity to source would lead us to expect. John the Baptist's crucial role in the Mass, as symbolic transition point between the Old Law and the New, places his pageant outside the domain of the improviser.

Then, introduced by a brattle of stanzas perhaps by the Wakefield Master himself, come the five great black pageants dealing with Christ's capture, trial, and death. Only one of the five, the *Coliphizacio*—the most brilliant of the five and one of the most brilliant pageants in the cycle—is all definitely the work of the Wakefield Master. Only here, among the five pageants, does ironic allegory and complex symbolism carry a large part of the meaning. But all five pageants have in common one feature which makes them powerful on stage. Though comic, in the Dantesque sense, since the audience knows that right will ultimately triumph and that the villains of the play will eventually get what they deserve, the pageants present all Christ's enemies as cunning, bloodthirsty, demonic figures, sadistic to the bone and insanely happy in their sadism. The characters who cause and delight in Christ's death appear in one pageant after another, pulling the strings: Pilate, Cayphas, Annas, and the torturers. Whereas Herod, with all his false and ludicrous pretensions, provokes scornful laughter, these villains, and especially Pilate—cleverer, more deadly, and more vicious than Herod—are designed to provoke much darker laughter—that of rage. Mahowne- or devil-worshiping Herod acted mainly from ludicrous fear. Pilate and his pals act from greed and, even more centrally, the witch's pleasure in evil. Here as in the Herod play, what makes the drama most terrible is the sharp and theatrical contrast between the very good and the very evil, and the apparent victory of the latter. In all these plays, the good enter— with sublime dignity—only to suffer while the evil come to cackle, rant, and dance.[2]

In the five-pageant sequence beginning with the *Conspiracio*, the evil characters are all, implicitly, devils, a foreshadowing of the literal devils who prance through the Harrowing of Hell. Pilate, in effect the chief enemy of Christ, is very much like Satan himself, and his war with Christ is the dramatic focus of the war of good and evil which orders the entire Wakefield *Corpus Christi* play. This idea, though fully developed by English pageant writers only in the Towneley MS cycle, derives from a venerable tradition. O. B. Hardison writes:

> For several reasons the liturgical forms adopted by the Carolingian bishops were particularly dramatic. Gustaf Aulen has shown in his *Christus Victor* that from the early fathers until the *Cur Deus homo?* of Anselm of Canterbury (1033–1109) a dramatic concept of the atonement prevailed in the Western Church. According to this view, the atonement is understood as an agon—a dramatic conflict between Christ and Satan culminating in the triumph of the Resurrection.[3]

Hardison has discussed this tradition, the Lenton agon, in some detail in the third essay of his *Christian Rite and Christian Drama in the Middle Ages,* and for full appreciation of the Towneley MS poet's theatrical realization of the Western "dramatic concept," the reader should see Hardison's essay. I will limit myself here to the way the Towneley MS plays work.

In the *Conspiracio,* which opens the series, the most interesting section is the beginning, Pilate's speech, written in the nine-line stanzas of the Wakefield Master, with alliterating long lines and (for the most part) metrically correct five-line conclusions. Pilate's lines seem, at first glance, to be much like Herod's in *Magnus Herodes.* Certainly they echo Herod's lines and were written with the Herod speech in mind. Pilate boasts of his power and talks of "great Mahowne." But there are differences. For one thing, the language and imagery of Pilate's threats is more dignified, hence more threatening. Whereas Herod addresses his listeners as "brodels" (wretches) and attacks his enemies with such phrases as "let thame go hang theme" and "I breke ilka bone," etc., (*MH*, 81, 84), Pilate speaks like an evil lord sure of his power:

> Peas, carles, I commaunde / vnconanad I call you;
> I say stynt and stande / or foull myght befall you.
> ffro this burnyshyd brande / now when I behald you,
> I red ye be shunand / or els the dwill skald you,
>   At onys.
> I am kyd, as men knawes,

leyf leder of lawes;
Seniours, seke to my sawes,
ffor bryssyng of youre bonys.

(*Consp.*, 1–9)

His choice of "carles" suggests imperatorial scorn rather than mere abuse (later, however, he uses Herod's word—e.g., line 571); his "burnyshyd brande" is more to be dreaded than Herod's blackjack scepter; and though the phrases "the dwill skald you" and "ffor bryssyng of youre bonys" might as easily have come from Herod, Pilate nowhere slips to the level of "I clefe / you small as flesh to pott" (*MH*, 98–99). Like Herod, Pilate is a friend of Mahowne, devil-figure for medieval poets; Herod claims to be Mahowne's cousin, while Pilate claims, more loftily, to be his grandsire (12). Pilate is a man more evil than Herod, for whereas Herod delights in and viciously defends his pretensions to power, claiming, among other things, that in him "standys lyfe and dede" (*MH*, 92) and that he must therefore be obeyed, Pilate's parallel claim (*Consp.*, 19) leads him to reveal his pleasure (exactly that of Fortune) in one moment supporting a man and, the next, destroying him, merely from evil whimsy:

ffor I am he that may / make or mar a man,
My self if I it say / as men of cowrte now can;
Supporte a man to day / to-morn agans hym than,
On both parties thus I play / And fenys me to ordan
    The right.

(19–23)

His pleasure, in short, is not in right as he understands it, nor is it entirely in personal power, but in *wrong*. Thus he adds:

Bot al fals indytars,
Quest mangers and Iurers,
And all thise fals out rydars,
    Ar welcom to my sight.

(24–27)

Since Christ is out, as Pilate says, to "dystroy oure law" (38) (i.e., trust in Fortune, the religion of hell), and since Pilate cannot get him honestly, he decides to get him by "sleyghts" (41). He reports

Christ's claims—that he represents the Trinity and so forth—and, instead of justifying himself by denying those claims, he says simply,

> If this be true in deyd,
> his shech [sect? speech?] shall spryng and sprede,
> And ouer com euer ylkone.

(51–53)

Here the nine-line Wakefield stanzas end (the last of these, starting at line 46, has a missing line), the remainder of the play being written in a variety of stanza forms, mostly four- and eight-line stanzas and couplets with a few recurrences of Wakefield stanzas or near equivalents. Generally speaking, Pilate is, for the rest of this pageant, a minor character, one of several wicked plotters and less interesting (to us) even than Christ lecturing and praying among his disciples.

Pilate's opening speech, one discovers, is not really necessary to the plot of the play. The action might have begun—and probably did begin, in an older version which is largely preserved in this revision —with Cayphas's entrance and opening speech to Pilate. Why did the Wakefield Master (or someone else) add the opening monologue? And, one must add, are the Wakefield stanzas which occasionally occur later in the play (at lines 617 and 643) and perhaps, also, the thirteen-line stanzas with short five-line conclusions like Wakefield-stanza conclusions—are these, too, as Pollard thought, the work of a late reviser? These questions are involved in one still more urgent: considering the stability of religious traditions (one of the premises of the principle of fidelity to source which partly governs the improvisation of medieval playwrights), why does the poet alter the traditional view of Pilate as merely a weak and mistaken man for this much darker figure?[4]

We may start with this: two points may be noted concerning all of the more complex stanzas. First, in them and seldom elsewhere in the pageant we find realistic detail of the kind which has been admired in the pageants of the York Metrist and the Wakefield Master. For example, the thirteen-line stanza beginning at line 600 closes as follows:

> Go we now on oure way,
> oure mastres for to may;
> Oure lantarnes take with vs alsway,
> And loke that thay be light!

(609–12)

The lanterns (introduced by Pilate at line 598) give a realistic touch not only as literal images but also as they reveal the fear the soldiers have of meeting Christ in the dark. (In later pageants in this tragic-phase group, Christ is viewed by his enemies as a witch.)

A second point to be noted concerning the Wakefield stanzas and their thirteen-line near equivalents is that it is chiefly here that exegetical jokes appear, and also chiefly here that the devil worship of the villains including the Wakefield cycle's strange new Pilate, is made explicit. Consider the nine-line stanza beginning at 617. The stanza closes with what appear to be two ironic exegetical jokes, one on Christ-as-bread (the Body bitten into), one on prayer ("boyne") to the Lord; and the stanza has, moreover, language of the colloquial kind normal in the late Wakefield pageants:

> ffor, as euer ete I breede,
> or I styr in this stede
> I wold stryke of his hede;
>   lord, I aske that boyne.
>
> (622–25)

In the next stanza, a thirteen-liner, Pilate's three knights claim they could bind their lord the devil (claiming for themselves, incidentally, a feat Christ will in fact perform); and in the next nine-liner (643sq.), Pilate affirms the same religion: "Sir Lucyfer the feynde / he lede you the trace!" (650–51). Exegetical jokes like those favored by the Wakefield Master do of course appear outside the nine- and thirteen-line stanzas—for instance, in the stanza beginning at line 150 (an eight-line stanza, tetrameter, *abababab*), where Pilate says, "that shall he [Christ] by [buy], by mahouns blode!" (157). The explanation is surely that here, as in the *Mactacio Abel* and in later plays also borrowed from York, the reviser has at times introduced his ideas into the older text, significantly altering a few words or adding a few lines. It may be noted in passing that colloquial phrases common in the Wakefield Master's plays also occur in eight-line (non-Wakefield) stanzas here, for example, "The dwill, he hang you high to dry!" (162; cf. *MA*, 13). The demonic characterization of Garcio may be a theatrical idea the poet executed after demonizing the tragic phase pageants. If so Garcio echoes Pilate, not the reverse.

Remove from the *Conspiracio* all nine- and thirteen-line stanzas and what remains is a pageant—mostly in plodding verse padded with lines thrown in for rhyme ("take hede vnto my sawe" [579])—

in which the stock villains, Cayphas, Annas, Pilate, Judas, and Mal-
chus, aided by cruel toadies, plot against and capture Christ; and
in which stock good people, Christ and his disciples, talk and pray.
The only theatrical action in the pageant is the cutting off of Mal-
chus's ear by Peter. The characterization of Pilate in this hypothetical pageant is the stock treatment found in the early mysteries—a
far cry, of course, from the sensitive and sympathetic treatment of
Pilate in the York Tapiteres and Couchers' pageant. Pilate's refusal
to murder Christ is unmotivated, in our hypothetical version; he
simply says, when the murder is suggested, "I will not assent vnto
youre saw; / I can ordan well better red" (726–27), a speech reflect-
ing the more honorable, traditional Pilate, and he sends Christ to
Cayphas, passing the buck. Reintroduce the nine- and thirteen-line
stanzas and Pilate and his friends become devil worshipers, Pilate
being the most terrible of all; Pilate's seeming change of heart in
sending Christ to Cayphas becomes part of his sadistic whimsy ("On
both parties thus I play" [22]); and the pageant becomes crueler
and more realistic in the sense that the evil characters are now more
convincing, because of their colloquial (late-style) diction, and live
in a world more concrete.

In the next pageant in the series, the *Coliphizacio,* Christ goes
before Cayphas and Annas for religious trial—a burlesque witch trial
in which Christ is viewed as witch and the witches play judge.
Though the pageant deserves much closer attention, my present object—to show the interrelationship of the five-pageant sequence—
forces me to treat it rather briefly.

Christ is an enemy to the "law"—religion—of the torturers, Cayphas, and Annas. He works, in their view, by something like magic:

> Sich wyles can thou make,
> Gar the people farsake
> Oure lawes, and thyne take;
> Thus art thou broght in blonder.

> (15–18)

He has made men mistakenly consider him a saint (20) and teaches
them "lege lawes new" (21); he has threatened to destroy their temple (73), he magically cures people for money (82–83), he raises the
dead, defiles the sabbath (84–85); in short, he practices "wychcraft"
(103) and may be called, as Cayphas calls him, a "mare" (nightmare)
(310). Cayphas and the rest swear throughout by their god, Satan:

"Speke on oone word, right in the dwyllys name!" Cayphas cries
(145); "the dwill gif the shame" (148, 163), "the dwill gyf hym
care!" (308), and so on.

The comedy in this system is typical Wakefield Master comedy, in
which carnality parodies spirituality, earth's rules burlesque heaven's.
One is the realm of illusion—in this case false religion, worship of
the devil, "God of the ground"[5]—the other the realm of truth. The
contrast of illusion and reality is supported by two main systems
of imagery: animal imagery in which Christ is a workhorse and his
tormenters are foxes or dogs and chickens; and game imagery, in
which Christ (by implication) does real work and his enemies play
games.[6]

Driving him to the judges at the start of the pageant, one of the
torturers shouts, "Do io furth, io! and trott on apase!" The torturers' last lines are,

> 2 *Tortor.* Lyft thy feete, may thou not?
> *Froward.* Then nedys me do nott
> But com after and dryfe.
>
> (430–32)

Cayphas talks of "barking" on books (reading aloud), as if he were
a dog (308); the torturers talk of themselves as cocks: "If he stode
vpon loft, we must hop and dawnse / As cokys in a croft" (354–55).
As for the game imagery, it hardly needs comment. Torturing Christ,
the three torturers play Hot Cockles (397–414) and allude to the
Shrovetide game of throwing sticks at a cock (354–55) (cf. Professor
Cawley's note to these lines); Cayphas alludes to, apparently, the
"game" of setting up a King of the Fools (166; see Cawley's note)
and Froward alludes to ninepins (408). For Cayphas and Annas, justice itself is a game. ("Amuse yourself," one judge tells the other
at one point, 185). From the outset, Cayphas is eager to find grounds
for condemnation: real justice is of no concern. Upon seeing Christ,
his first words to the torturers are:

> Say, were ye oght adred?
> Were ye oght wrang led,
> Or in any strate sted?
> Syrs, who has myscaryd?
>
> (51–54)

Annas, on the other hand, at first seems honestly concerned with
truth. He asks cautiously; making sure the testimony is sound, "Say,
were ye oght in dowte for fawte of light / As ye wached therowte?"
(55–56). (The exegetical quibble on *light* is a typical Wakefield Master joke.) And later in the pageant, out of his concern for the rules,
Annas repeatedly cautions his fellow against being "irregulere" (306).
His concern is not justice, however, but mere legalism—and sometimes worse. He says at one point, "It is best that we trete hym
with farenes." Cayphas answers, "We, nay!" And Annas explains his
reason: "And so myght we gett hym som word for to say" (217–18).

The chief ways in which the playwright comments in theatrical
terms on the illusion-reality contrast are in his use of the suffering
servant, Froward, and his handling of the character Christ. Poor
miserable Froward is one of many persecuted servants in the work
of the Wakefield Master. (With *Col.*, 300–383, compare the complaints
of Garcio, in *Mactacio Abel*, 418–39; Slawpase in *Prima Pastorum*,
192–201; Daw in *Secunda Pastorum*, 154–71). But Froward's function
in the pageant seems to go beyond social criticism to grotesque Christological parody. In his service to the torturer he does for them what
they cannot do or are afraid to do (as Christ does for man what
man cannot do himself). Froward goes close enough to give Christ
the stool, after which the torturers must ask Christ to sit, being
afraid to force him (361), and Froward puts the blindfold on Christ,
goes to get the whips, and so on. In a ludicrous, strictly physical
sense, Froward is the torturers' "savior." On the other hand, in the
whipping games, he plays judge. "I stode and beheld—thou towchid
not the skyn / Bot fowll" (400–401): "Yei, that was well gone to; /
Ther start vp a cowll" (404–5). In his ninepins allusion, "I can my
hand vphefe and knop out the skalys" (408), there may be, I think,
an exegetical joke on Christ's raising his hand (in the court of Last
Judgment) to "knock out" or set aside the scales of good and evil
deeds, allowing the sinner who calls on his mercy to pass. If this
interpretation of Froward is right, we may add that the poet emphasizes the strictly physical limit of Froward's saving and judging
powers. Complaining against bringing Christ a stool (a parodic
throne?), Froward says, "For the wo that he shall dre, / Let him
knele on his kne" (348–49), lines which suggest, ironically, another
kind of kneeling—prayer for spiritual help. When the torturers tell
Froward that they want the stool because Christ, with his great
height and manliness, might make them dance like cocks if they
were to allow him to stand while beating him, Froward answers,
rather obscurely,

> Now a veniance
> Come on hym!
> Good skill can ye shew
> As fell i the dew.

(355–58)

His meaning seems to be (as Professor Cawley puts it) "that the reason given by the First Torturer for asking him to bring a stool (353–55) is no more substantial than the dew."[7] But the lines perhaps have also a spiritual sense that Froward is too carnal to understand. What came into the world as mysteriously as dew, as all good medieval Christians understood, was the immaculately conceived Christ. (Cf. the lyric, *I Syng a Mayden þat is Makeles.*) What saves man is really not reason but the Incarnation.

I need not point out that this view of Froward is speculative or, anyway, subjective. There might be no such limitation if we could watch the original performance. There is no reason that Froward and Christ might not be similarly dressed or that pageant actors might not use symbolic gesture just as priests did in performing the Mass; no reason, for instance, that Froward might not extend his arms in grimacing parody of the Crucifixion while delivering the lines, "In fayth, syr, we had almost / Knokyd hym on slepe" (422–23), just as, in the words of Bishop Durandus, "The celebrant therefore, representing this [the Crucifixion] while speaking of the blessed Passion, extends his hands in the manner of a cross" (*Rationale*, IV, xliii, 3). It is clear, at all events, that Christological parody does occur in the mysteries—in the burlesque feast of *Prima Pastorum*, Mak's sheep in *Secunda Pastorum*, and in Herod, later Pilate within the "tragic-phase" pageants.

The single most remarkable and most impressive thing about the *Coliphizacio* is the playwright's handling of Christ. He almost never speaks (he says four lines, 251–54); he moves slowly when he moves at all and, for the most part, he stands still; yet he is the dramatic center of the play. Cayphas dances about, screams, curses, frustrated by Christ's silence (127–80, et passim); Annas wheedles (238–50); the torturers whip him; but all their activity is, for Christ, senseless farce. His silence and motionlessness are the pageant's dramatic comment on what is real, what illusory or passing.

Pilate appears again, speaking the opening lines of the third pageant in the series, the *Fflagellacio*. His words, presented in the the thirteen-line near equivalent of the Wakefield stanza, recall, almost phrase by phrase, his opening speech in the *Conspiracio*. There can be no doubt that the poet has the earlier speech in mind. There he said "ffro this burnyshyd brande / now when I behald you, I red ye be shunand" (Consp., 3-4) here he says, "Wtih this brande that I bere ye shall bytterly aby" (F, 4). There he talked of his conscious and joyful falsehood (Consp., 19-27) and swore he would get Christ by "sleyghtys" (Consp., 41); here he states at once:

> I am full of sotelty,
> falshed, gyll, and trechery;
> Therfor am I namyd by clergy
>   As mali actoris.
>
>   (F, 10-13)

He brags here, as in the earlier pageant, of his greed, saying he is glad to help the side of right if he may get thereby some advantage (16-17), and adds, echoing his statement of his inconstancy in the Conspiracio, "Then to the fals parte I turne me agayn" (F, 18). Pilate directly echoes his statement in the Conspiracio that—

> all fals indytars,
> Quest mangers and Iurers,
> And all thise fals out rydars,
> Ar welcom to my sight
>
>   (Consp., 24-27)

when he says in the Fflagellacio,

> All fals endytars,
> Quest gangars, and Iurars,
> And thise out-rydars
>   Ar welcom to me.
>
>   (F, 23-26)

The point should need no further laboring. The Pilate of the Flagellation pageant is the same Pilate met in the Conspiracy pageant, and he serves the same god, Lucifer-Mahowne:

> ye men that vse bak-bytyngys,
> and rasars of slanderyngys,
> ye ar my dere darlyngys,
>   And mahowns for euermore.
>
>   (36-39)

The torturers met in the *Coliphizacio*—afraid of Christ, always keeping their distance, but delighted as children playing a game by the
pain they can inflict on him—are the same torturers who reappear
here. In the *Coliphizacio* the torturers made their servant blindfold
Christ, they themselves being afraid of him, and Cayphas, striking
at Christ and missing, complained "Syr, why standys he so far?"
(*Col.*, 299); here, when they are trying to tie him to a pillar, one
asks the other the same question: "why standys thou so far?" (131).
In that play they played games and danced or feared that Christ
would make *them* dance (*Col.*, 354); here the third torturer tells
Christ "I shall lede the a dawnce" (80), and the first tells Christ,
later, "Com on! tryp on thi tose / without any fenyng" (224). In
the Wakefield stanza which closes the *Fflagellacio,* the torturers show
the same joy in evil that they showed throughout the *Coliphizacio,*
and they end with a chase image which recalls animal imagery in
the earlier pageants and closely echoes two lines in *Coliphizacio,*
431–32.

> *Tercius tortor.* Now by mahowne, oure heuen kyng,
>   I wold that we were in that stede
> where we myght hym on cros bryng.
>   Step on before, and furth hym lede
>   A trace.
> *primus tortor.* Com on thou!
> *iius tortor.* Put on thou!
> *iijus tortor.* I com fast after you,
>   And folowse on the chace.
>
>   (408–16)

The pageant comes close in many ways to the cruel dazzle of the
Coliphizacio: in its characterization of the demonic tormenters, in
its textural richness, and in its dramatic economy. In one respect
it recalls the *Magnus Herodes* and carries the dark effect achieved
there even further. After the sadistic jokes of the torturers in the
pageant's first movement there comes a lyrical second movement in
which the gentleness and dignity of John, the holy women, and
Christ contrast with the grisly stuff that has gone before. At the end
of this passage, the torturers turn shrilly on Christ and the women,
and then on Simon of Cyrene. Against the lyricism and the slow
pace of the interlude the playwright sets not only the torturers' rant
but also the fretful hastening of Simon, who is bound on a long
journey he thinks terribly important, a journey which will not allow

him to help Christ carry the cross. Good Simon's words to the torturers curiously play on traditional associations with the Crucifixion,
much as the wicked Froward's words and actions played on the nature of Christ. The great journey he must make "this same day"
(363–64) seems to play on the long journey Christ must take, to heaven ("This day you will be with me in Paradise"); Simon's plea that
he "shall com full soyn agane, / To help this man with all my mayn"
(384–85) seems to play on the idea of the Second Coming; his claim
that "that were vnwysely wroght, / To beytt me bot if I respast oght
/ Aythere in worde or dede" play on the condemnation of Christ
though he is without fault; and Simon's statement that "To help this
man I am well payde" (401) has clear overtones that Simon himself
does not understand—paid with salvation. In the dramatically irrelevant good character Simon, as in the minor if not irrelevant bad
character Froward in the earlier play, the poet establishes his ironic
comment on the antics of the impish torturers and their demonic
masters.

The last two pageants in the sequence, *Processus Crucis* and *Processus Talentorum,* need no detailed discussion. The first contains
only one Wakefield stanza, no better or worse than the more conventional stanzas around it; and the whole pageant contains—and,
given its subject, needs—no allegory. If the lines are generally un-
inspired, nothing can be more theatrical than nailing a wise and
gentle man to a cross, mocking him, and watching him gush blood
(from a goatskin bag in original production). Pilate, who opens the
pageant, and the torturers, who are central figures within it, speak
and behave much as they do in the earlier pageants, though without
the bright flashes of imagery and without the exegetical jokes. Christ
speaks in conformity with the medieval style in the Crucifixion pageant, calling attention to his wounds, comforting, and forgiving. The
pageant's greatest virtue is the rhythmic alternation of gentle scenes
and lines with demonic comedy.[8]

In other words, the text is dull, though the pageant, on stage, was
no doubt overwhelming. It is the darkest pageant in the whole
Towneley MS: it begins with Pilate's tyrannical rant ("by mahownys
bloode"), wrings the emotions of Christ's friends, mocks those emotions with the torturers' prattle, and ends with Joseph and Nicode-
mus carrying the dead body of Christ to its tomb.

The five-pageant series closes with the *Talentorum.* Like the *Conspiracio,* the *Fflagellacio,* and the *Processus Crucis,* it opens with a
speech by Pilate, this time five Wakefield stanzas and a variant, mostly

in Latin. In solemn language suggestive of the Black Mass, with threats that sound not amusing but dead serious, Pilate commands silence, states his lineage and the credentials of his power, and warns that those who defy his law will be executed. Then, one after another, the three torturers rush in, each gleefully boasting—with exegetical jokes—of his extraordinary wickedness. The first squeals:

> war, war! for now com I,
> The most shrew in this cuntry;
> I haue ron full fast in hy,
>   hedir to this towne;
> To this towne now comen am I
> ffrom the mownt of caluery;
> Ther crist hang, and that full hy,
>   I swe[re] you, by my crowne.
>
>   (83–90)

By "crowne" the braggart of course means pate; he'll get no other. In his next stanza he boasts of spitting on Christ's face, shiny as it was already (83)—a nasty halo joke. He and his friends, he says, stripped Christ's clothing and nailed him to the cross. He now comes to Pilate to see which of the torturers will get Christ's clothes,

> ffor whosoeuer may get thise close,
> he ther neuer rek where he gose,
> ffor he semys nothyng to lose,
>   If so be he theym were . . .
>
>   (105–8)

—apparently another exegetical joke: in the radiant apparel of God (in the New Jerusal) one has everything. The second torturer rushes in, half crazy th joy but fearful that he may have come too late. He too brag nat he is "The most shrew, that dar I swere, / That ye shall fynd aw where" (122–23) and claims that he taught Christ a new game, one in which Christ lays down his head, after which "I bobyd hym on the crowne" (131). Like the first torturer, he is after Christ's clothes. If he can, he will "both drynke and ete" (143)—wine and bread, presumably—"as I were made" (144). The third torturer comes, running so fast he has broken, he says, "both my balok stones" (147). He is as bad as the others, "the most shrew in all myn kyn" (154), and has come to start, with the others, a new "game" (158), that of dividing up Christ's coat. Though they worry that he may cheat them, the torturers go before Pilate. Pilate does indeed want the coat, as they suspected he would, and when he can't win it by a lucky roll of dice, he gets it from the third torturer by threats. In the Wakefield stanzas which close the pageant, the three torturers irrelevantly forswear dice (it was Pilate—a figure of Fortune—not the mere dice, that beat them), blaming on dice all the evils of the world. Turning his back on dice, the stupid third torturer comes for wrong reasons to a right conclusion:

> I red leyf sich vayn thyng / and serue god herafter,
>   ffor heuens blys;
> That lord is most myghty,
> And gentyllyst of Iury,
>   we helde to hym holy;
>   how thynk y by this?
>
> (398–403)

Pilate, who knows the difference between winning and losing (in a carnal sense anyway), and knows very well how he got Christ's coat, laughs and praises the torturers' wisdom. "Of all the clerkys that I knaw, most conyng ye be," he tells them, and he admires the "soteltes of youre sawes" (405–6). He promises to continue their good friend and, quoting French like Herod, bids them good-day. The sly antagonist of Christ throughout the whole five pageant sequence has triumphed, it seems, not only over Christ but over his own evil stooges as well. He leaves them with Mahowne's blessing (410–11).

In the Towneley MS, as in no other mystery cycle that has come down to us, all the events from the conspiracy to the Crucifixion and the gaming for Christ's robe are developed as a battle between two figures, Pilate and Christ, in which Christ appears to lose and Pilate seems to win. The opening speeches in four of the pageants make Pilate the evil motive force, Christ the victim; and in the one pageant which Pilate does not introduce, the lesser henchmen of Lucifer-Mahowne, Cayphas and Annas, are forced to turn the matter over to Pilate. The pageants are drawn together by central motifs and images—devil worship, games, animals—by consistent characterization of the evil forces, and by exegetical jokes of the kind favored by the Wakefield Master. The appearance of Wakefield stanzas or close variants in all the pageants need not be taken as a sign that the Wakefield Master himself wrote and/or revised these pageants. (Wakefield stanzas, after all, appear in the York cycle—see the Brocheres' play, *Mortificacio Cristi*.) But in the Towneley MS, where most of the best pageants can be assigned to one man—the *Processus Noe cum Filiis*, the *Secunda Pastorum*, the *Magnus Herodes*, and the *Coliphizacio*—the appearance of that man's stanza form strongly suggests either the hand of that playwright or conscious imitation of his method. And the example of the *Mactacio Abel*, where we see the Wakefield Master at work as a reviser, keeping some older material and adding some new material, gives precedent for the kind of revision I am suggesting must have operated here in whole five-pageant sequence of the *Corpus Christi* play's "tragic phase." Fundamentally, what the five-pageant sequence has in common with the pageants we assign to the Wakefield Master is the premise that earth burlesques heaven. As Mak is a false (illusory, carnal) God figure in *Secunda Pastorum* and the sheep he steals is a false Christ child, so here Satan-Mahowne is a false God figure and Pilate, his vicegerent, is a false Christ-as-King.

TEN

The Comic Triumph:
From the Deliverance
to the Judgment

The "recognition and reversal" in the *Corpus Christi* play comes in two pageants, the Harrowing of Hell, in which Christ overcomes his old enemy the devil, and the Resurrection, in which that victory is dramatized for man by the open tomb.[1] As Professor Hardison says, "The end, or the epiphany, extends from the appearances of Christ to the disciples to the Last Judgment."[2] It goes without saying that if the reversal and close of the huge, multipageant play are to be powerful, they must conclude what has actually gone before, recalling earlier moments of the Christ-Satan struggle for the souls of all mankind—the "corpus Christi." In the Wakefield play, more strikingly than in any other English *Corpus Christi* cycle, the close has been designed to fit what comes before.

The *Extraccio Animarim* and the *Resurreccio Domini* in the Wakefield cycle are both borrowed from York and skillfully revised. What the Wakefield poet chiefly expands in the Harrowing play is the scenes involving devils.[3] In one instance after another, the reviser's alterations recall earlier devices in the Wakefield *Corpus Christi* play. For example, where he finds in York the lines,

> *Sattan* What page is þere þat makes prees,
> And callis hym kyng of vs in fere?

> (Y., 125–26)

the Wakefield poet writes,

> *Rybald.* Out, harro, out! what devill is the
> That callys hym kyng ouer vs all?
>
> (T., 116–17)

The change is slight but significant. Whereas the York version plays ironically on "page" and "kyng," in Wakefield Rybald's speech makes Christ's words the call of a king of devils (which, in an ironic sense, Christ is). The York verbal play is sacrificed for two higher effects, realistic characterization of Rybald (in which this shift is a minor detail) and reflection of the poet's (or poets') repeated treatment of Christ, earlier in the Wakefield cycle, as a witch, nightmare (*Coliphizacio,* 310), or devil-figure in the upside-down religion. The word "hedusly" (T., 110) reinforces this; in the York source the first devil's line "For hydously I herde hym calle" (Y., 138) comes several lines later and has no such effect, telling us merely that the first devil is frightened.

Not at all surprisingly, Satan's lines, and sometimes Belzabub's, recall in the Wakefield pageant the boasts and threats made for or by Herod, Pilate, and the lesser tyrants. For example, with the whole *nuncius* speech in *Magnus Herodes,* and especially with "ffree men are his thrall," (*MH,* 55–56), compare—

> *Belzabub.* honowre! harsto, harlot, for what dede?
> Alle erthly men to me ar thrall.
>
> (*Extraccio,* 136–37)

The poet dilates on this idea of tyrants as burlesques of the King of Kings in Herod's long speech and again in the two Pilate speeches which directly echo Herod's, *Conspiracio,* 1–19, and *Fflagellacio,* 1–8. In the present case the boast comes from the York source, line 134, where it is spoken not by Belzabub but by Satan. In the Wakefield version, Satan himself also echoes Herod and the rest, and does so in lines not found in the York version. Compare two typical speeches demanding silence, the first by Herod, the second by Pilate, with lines spoken by Satan, introduced into the Wakefield revision of the York text.

> *Herod:*
> Peasse both yong and old at my bydyng, I red,
> For I haue all in wold: in me standys lyfe and dede;
> Who that is so bold, I brane hym thrugh the hede!
>
> (*MH,* 91–93)

Pilate:
>   Peasse I byd euereich Wight!
>   Stand as styll as stone in Wall,
>   Whyls ye ar present in my sight,
>   That none of you clatter ne call
> ffor if ye do, youre dede is dight
>   I warne it you both greatt and small,
>   With this brand burnyshyd so bright,
>   Therfor in peasse loke ye be all.

>   (*Proc. Crucis,* 1–8)

Sathanas. The devill you all to-har!
>   What ales the so to showte?
>   And me, if I com nar,
>   thy brayn bot I bryst owte!

>   (*Extraccio,* 142–45)

We hear similar threats, as we have noted before, from Garcio in *Mactacio Abel.* In all these speeches, by the way, hanging is a favorite threat—a detail not common in other cycles and probably traceable to the Wakefield poet's special interest in social satire or realism. Satan's mind, too, runs to hangings, but here in the sense of crucifixion. He tells Rybald, in *Extraccio,* line 216, "yee, hangyd be thou on a cruke."

Let me pause here for some observations. Some of the *Extraccio* pageant's echoes of earlier pageants in the Towneley MS come from the York source, as I have noted, but in the York play they do not function as they do here. Recall that the Pilate speech introduced by the Wakefield poet at the beginning of the older Conspiracy play, the closely parallel Pilate speech which begins the Wakefield *Fflagellacio,* the highly irregular Pilate speech which begins the Wakefield *Processus Crucis,* and the Latin-English Pilate speech which opens the Wakefield pageant of the Talents are *all* intrusive, that is, they are inserted by the Wakefield reviser and involve a shift from the stock characterization of Pilate to one not found in any other mystery cycle, English or Continental.[4] In other words, though Mahowne-Satan worship is a commonplace of the English cycles, and though the characterization of Herod as bully is standard, only in the Wakefield cycle do we find this chiming repetition, in pageant after pageant, of the same idea: tyrants silencing men by cutting off their heads, breaking their bones,

or hanging them high, and only here is the insistence on the demonism
of the tyrants so emphatic.

For his *Extraccio* the Wakefield playwright made numerous other
changes in the York pageant he used. (For a full list see Pollard's introduction.) He drops the first quatrain of York stanza 16, substituting
the more impressive Latin cry of Christ (*"Attollite portas, principes,
vestras et eleuamini portae eternales, et introibit rex gloriae"* [115]), a
cry the poet has Christ use again, like a magician's spell, at line 184.
Something of Christ's miraculous power—his "magic"—is present in
the York version, in Christ's sending the light ahead of him to hell,
but his mysterious power is underscored and dramatized in the Wakefield pageant. In the York version Christ calls Michael to bind Satan,
using force, not magic. The call to Michael is deleted in the Wakefield
pageant, which moves directly to Christ's "Deville, I commaunde the
to go downe / Into thi sete where thou shalle syt" (357–58) and Satan's
fall. All of these details recall the treatment of first Moses, type of
Christ, and then Christ himself, as a witch. (Moses at line 232 of
Pharao is a "warlow"; Christ is accused of witchcraft in *Coliphizacio*,
103.)

This change in the characterization of Christ is inextricably involved with another great change, the poet's new characterization of
Satan. In the York version Satan simply confronts Christ, argues texts,
and loses, then tries force and loses to Michael and to Christ's command. The Wakefield Satan is a far more appealing demon, half
heroic, half absurd. He is, like the York Satan, supremely confident,
and to throw this confidence into sharp relief, the Wakefield poet
creates the easily terrified imp, Rybald, and adds new dimensions to
the nobler demon, Belzabub. At the first signs of Christ's attack, Rybald squeals (lines not in York),

> Sen fyrst that hell was mayde And I was put therin,
>   Sich sorow neuer ere I had nor hard I sich a dyn;
> My hart begynnys to brade my wytt waxys thyn,
>   I drede we can not be glad thise saules mon fro
>   vs twyn.
>
> how, belsabub! bynde thise boys, sich harow was
>   neuer hard in hell.

(T., 89–93)

Belzabub, a far mightier devil, scoffs at Rybald's panic and calms him.
At the same time, Belzabub does not much underestimate the trouble.

He asks that war councillors be called together, including Satan himself. Rybald says, self-possessed again, "All redy lord I go." And then
comes the unearthly, booming voice of Christ, "*Attollite portas* . . ."
Poor Rybald is shattered, half out of his wits:

> Out, harro, out! what devill is he
>   That callys hym kyng ouer vs all?
> hark belzabub, com ne,
>   ffor hedusly I hard hym call!
>
> (T., 116–19)

Again Belzabub calms him:

> Go, spar the yates, yll mot thou the!
>   And set the waches on the wall;
> If that brodell com ne
>   With vs ay won he shall;
>
> And if he more call or cry,
>   To make vs more debate,
> lay on hym hardely,
>   And make hym go his gate.
>
> (T., 120–27)

David solemnly delivers the Old Testament comment: Christ will win.
Belzabub hurls abuse at him, insisting on his power—"All erthly men
to me ar thrall" (137)—but can spare no time for debate. The walls
are cracking; the captives in Limbo are arising. Belzabub calls out,
"how, sir sathanas! com nar / And hark this cursid rowte!" But when
Christ brings down hell's castle walls, opening Limbo, Satan is reclin-
ing complacently in his inner chamber. Rybald cries

> lymbo is lorne, alas!
> sir sathanas com vp;
>   This wark is wars then it was!
>
> (213–15)

(With line 215, compare *Secunda Pastorum*, line 119.)

Now Satan is furious, convinced that the catastrophe is the fault of
his sluggard army. To Rybald he howls,

yee, hangyd be thou on a cruke!

Thefys, I bad ye shuld be bowne,
  If he maide mastres more,
To dyng that dastard downe,
  sett hym both sad and sore!

(T., 216–20)

But Belzabub has seen Christ's strange power, his ability to bring down the very gates of hell with mere words, and he angrily scoffs,

To sett hym sore, that is sone saide!
  com thou thi self and serue hym so;
we may not abyde his bytter brayde,
  he wold vs mar and we were mo.

(T., 221–24; cf. Y., 205–8)

As in the York version, Satan throws on his armor and goes up to deal with the "belamy" upstart. In the flyting which ensues—the traditional Anglo-Saxon verbal dual—Satan comes to see, with increasing alarm, that he misjudged his man. As in York, he begins to wheedle, first asking Christ to leave at least a few souls, then begging Christ to take him to heaven too, if he must free all the souls. When Christ says he will leave only the evil—Cain and his like—and will send other evil souls not yet born, Satan is delighted. He says (following the York source) he will walk where he pleases, a great lord. Christ answers, "Nay feynde, thou shalbe feste, / that thou shall flyt no far" (353–54), and Satan, horrified by the thought, leaps at Christ, howling "thou shalbe smytt!" "I commaunde the to go downe," Christ says, and the devil, amazed, begins sinking. In York, at this point, Satan calls for help from Mahowne; but there is no such hope in the Towneley MS version. The poet cuts directly to "Alas, for doyll and care! / I synk into hell pyt!" (359–60). In all this the Wakefield poet drew heavily on his York sources, but finally the characterization of Satan is his own.

    The next pageant in the closing group in the Wakefield *Corpus Christi* is the *Resurreccio Domini,* another pageant borrowed from York. The pageant opens, like four of the pageants in the tragic movement, with an intrusive speech by Pilate, whom we have already recognized as the satanic control of the tragic action. Irregular stanzas

appear throughout the pageant, suggesting revision or new material
where we cannot compare the writing with a known source, as, for
instance, we cannot do in the case of Cayphas's speech at lines 37–44.
New stanzas are in general highly dramatic and rich in concrete
imagery; see, for instance, the largely intrusive Centurian speech,
lines 45–75. There are many other changes, particularly toward the
end of the pageant, where cutting and a redistribution of lines completely changes the characterization of Cayphas and Annas. In the
York pageant, the weak but relatively sympathetic Pilate turns to
Cayphas:

> *Pil.*　　Sir Cayphas, ʒe are a connyng clerke,
> If we amisse haue tane oure merke
> 　　I trowe same faile,
> þerfore what schalle worþe nowe of þis werke?
> 　　Sais your counsaille.
>
> 　　　　　　　　　　　　　　　　　(Y., 396–400)

Cayphas answers:

> To saie þe beste forsothe I schall,
> That schall be prophete to vs all,
> ʒone knyghtis behoues þere wordis agayne call
> 　　Howe he is miste.
> We node for thyng þat myght be-fall
> 　　þat no man wiste.
>
> 　　　　　　　　　　　　　　　　　(Y., 401–6)

In the Towneley version Pilate asks, with no comment on Cayphas's
abilities,

> I pray you, Cayphas, ye vs wys
> 　　Of this enfray.
>
> 　　　　　　　　　　　　　　　　　(T., 528–29)

and Cayphas responds:

> Sir, and I couth oght by my clergys,
> 　　ffayn wold I say.
>
> 　　　　　　　　　　　　　　　　　(T., 530–31)

In this version it is Annas who has the answer—the answer which Cayphas gave in the York version:

> *Annas.*   To say the best for sothe I shall;
> It shalbe profett for vs all,
> yond knyghtys behovys thare wordys agane call
> how he is myst, *etc.*
>
> > (T., 532–35; cf. Y., 401–6 above)

Why these changes? If we look at Cayphas and Annas speeches earlier in the *Resurreccio* we discover that Cayphas is regularly the pressing questioner, Annas the pedantic commentor. Typical lines of Cayphas are: "Wonder yll? I pray the why? / declare that to this company" (86–87; from York, 61–62) and "we pray the tell vs, of what thyng?" (110; from York 85, there given to Annas). Cayphas's lines,

> 3a, sir, such reasouns may 3e rewe,
> 3e schulde noght neueyn such note enewe,
> But 3e couthe any tokenyngis trewe
> Vnto vs tell
>
> > (Y., 79–82)

are in the Towneley MS transferred to Annas (104 sq.). Scurrilous lines and ranting lines stay with Cayphas.

What all these facts together suggest is that the Wakefield reviser sees Cayphas as a blustering, violent, not very intelligent man, Annas as a man who wins by cunning and manipulation. That is, we recall, exactly the characterization of Cayphas and Annas in the tragic-phase plays, especially the *Coliphizacio,* where these two villains are central. In other words, the poet seems to have made all these changes in order to adapt the York pageant to the drama of the Wakefield *Corpus Christi* play as a whole.

The next three pageants can be dismissed in a few words.[5] The *Peregrini* has apparently been pieced together from many sources: it begins with seven-line stanzas linked by verbal repetition (*ken,* line 7, and *ken,* line 8; *blo,* line 14, and *blo,* line 15), a popular device in northern lyrics; after the apparently truncated third stanza, the pageant's only Wakefield stanza occurs, bringing in a new speaker, Luke; then comes a series of six-line stanzas (twelve of them) presenting a formal exchange, stanza by stanza, between Cleophus and Luke. After these, with Jesus' first speech, come two four-line stanzas, followed by more six-line stanzas of formal exchange between Cleophus, Luke, and Christ and so the pageant continues, highly irregular to the end, always shifting stanza forms just where new speakers or plot elements enter, exactly as if the pageant were put together by snipping together bits of older plays and lyrics. I think it is possible to separate out the various elements brought together from diverse sources and spliced to one another with original lines, but for my present purpose the undertaking would be unprofitable, partly because it is impossible to tell whether the collage was done in Wakefield or was borrowed as it stands, and partly because the pageant makes no great contribution to the *Corpus Christi* play as a whole; it merely gets through a plot necessity, Christ's reappearance to a few of his disciples.

Much the same may be said of *Thomas Indie:* a good, playable piece, excellent in places—Paul's antifeminist remarks, a fine dramatic irony here, since what Mary Magdalene says is in fact true; or Peter's wonderfully irrelevant words of remorse about his denial of Christ. The playwright may or may not have achieved this latter effect intentionally, but the effect is that, whatever the other characters may be saying, Peter cannot get his mind off his guilt. The individualization of Paul and Peter, who are both in some sense doubters at the outset— Paul because he distrusts women, Peter because he is preoccupied— beautifully, though perhaps accidentally, sets up the more serious doubt of Thomas. Peter's irrelevant lament is of course in a new meter, but there is no way of telling whether the poet intended the disjointed effect or got it simply by a scissors-and-paste shift from one source to another. In any case, there is no sign here of the Wakefield Master's genius with language and imagery. Like the *Peregrini,* the *Thomas* gets the job done, advancing the plot.

And the same may be said of the fragmentary third pageant in this group, the *Ascencio Domini,* again a pageant in many meters. All of these pageants afford possibilities of interesting spectacle, but this pageant, of course, gives the noblest possibilities of all. Professor Swart mentions the lines in which Christ calls, "Opyn the clowdes, for now I com / In joy and blys to dwell with the" (252–53); they are followed by the stage direction, "*& sic ascendit, cantantibus angelis 'Ascendo ad patrem meum.'* " Here, as in the Pilgrim and Thomas pageants, analysis of the structural blocks marked by meter shift suggests clever borrowing from several sources for a unique effect, but there are no proofs that the effects are intentional, not just lucky. When Pilate, in the *Fflagellacio,* echoes his own words in the *Conspiracio,* the poet's purpose is clear: he means the audience to make certain connections. But

juxtapositions of disparate materials which involve no rhetorical signaling, however fitting they may be, elude critical testing. If Christ's
triumph in the *Peregrini*, the *Thomas*, and the *Ascencio* is "tight,"
the tightness is theatrical, not textual. Satan's relationship with Herod,
Pilate, and the rest, on the other hand, is verbal.

The Wakefield *Judicium*—the crowning pageant of the Towneley
MS *Corpus Christi* play—has as its source the York Merceres' pageants;
it contains forty-two nine-line Wakefield stanzas undoubtedly written
by the Wakefield Master, and recalls, with a vengeance, all that has
gone before.

The beginning of the pageant is lost. The beginning we have,
though accidental, is so brilliant that one hopes not too much came
before. (There must have been at least one MS page.) One of the
wicked called to judgment [*Secundus Malus?*] whimpers, in internally
rhymed imperfectly alliterative lines analogous to those favored by the
Wakefield Master, about the dreadfulness of his situation. He closes
with a six-line stanza in a different meter, probably lifted from some
early play or lyric. The third wicked man (MS *Tercius malus*) laments
his mistakes in superb six-line stanzas clearly from another source. The
fourth laments in another stanza form, quasi-alliterative, like the beginning of the first speaker's lines. An angel enters, and then Christ,
and they speak in strong, apparently borrowed eight-line stanzas with
no snatches at rhyme or other imperfections common in early-style
pageant stanzas. After this, the devils speak. They use nine-line Wakefield stanzas rich in colloquial language and vivid imagery, full of
colloquial exclamations ("Oute, haro, out, out!" [89]) and always
evocative, often reacting to stage business—e.g., "harkyn to this horne"
(89). Characterization is deft, partly because of the Wakefield Master's
favorite trick of providing his characters—even the most minor—with
personal history. With the soliloquies of Coll, Gyb, and Daw in
Secunda Pastorum, or with Cayphas's cursing of his teacher back in
school (*Coliphizacio*, 307–8), compare:

> I was neuer in dowte or now at this morne;
> So sturdy a showte sen that I was borne
> hard I neuer here abowte in ernyst ne in skorne;
>   A wonder!
> I was bonde full fast
> In yrens for to last,
> Bot my bandys thai brast
>   And shoke all in sonder.

                                                              (90–97)

Besides the realistic diction signaling the hand of the Wakefield Master there is an at once local and eschatological joke, "let vs go to this dome vp watlyn strete" (126—"Watling Street" is sometimes used of the Milky Way), there are real-life comic allusions like the first devil's pilgrimage joke, "I had leuer go to rome, yei thryse, on my fete, / Then forto grefe yond grome or with hym forto mete" (128). Or compare:

> *primus demon.*
>   how so the gam crokys,
>   Examyn oure bokys.
> *secundus demon.* here is a bag full, lokys,
>   of pride and of lust
>
>   Of Wraggers and wrears a bag full of brefes,
>   Of carpars and cryars of mychers and thefes,
>   Of lurdans and lyars that no man lefys,
>   Of flytars, of flyars and renderars of reffys . . .
>
> (139–48)

The whole long exchange of the devils and Tutiuillus is full of social satire—on vain women, on foppish men who pad their shoulders, and so forth. And there are words like *nerehande* rarely or never found in the cycles outside the work of the Wakefield Master. Sometimes the satire is biting, angry in tone and vivid in imagery as is only the work of the Wakefield Master in the English mystery cycles. For instance:

> If she be neuer so fowll a dowde with her kelles and hir pynnes,
> The shrew hir self can shrowde both hir chekys and hir chynnes;
> she can make it full prowde with iapes and with gynnes,
> hir hede as hy as a clowde bot no shame of hir synnes
>   Thai fele;
> When she is thus paynt,
> she makes it so quaynte,
> She lookys like a saynt,
>   And wars then the deyle.
>
> (260–68)

The demonism which defined the evil characters of earlier pageants is recalled here, for instance in the lines by one of the wicked, "But oft tymes maide we sacrifice / to sathanas when othere can slepe" (23–24).

After line 385, the Wakefield stanzas momentarily give way to older
stanza forms in the lines spoken by Jesus, but as soon as the devils
re-enter the pageant (532) Wakefield stanzas recur, and echoes of the
Wakefield Master's diction, realistic but also metaphoric in calling up
analogous physical situations:

> *primus demon.*
> > Do now furthe go, trus, go we hyne!
> > vnto endles wo ay-lastand pyne;
> > Nay, tary not so we get ado syne.
> *secundus demon.* hyte hyder warde, no harry ruskyne!
> > > War oute!
> > The meyn shall ye nebyll,
> > And I shall syng the trebill,
> > A revant the devill
> > > Till all this holw rowte.
>
> > > > > > > (532–40)

With this passage compare the carter language (here shifted to bailey
language) of the opening and closing lines of the *Coliphizacio* and,
also, the jokes on singing in *Prima Pastorum,* lines 407–30, and *Secunda Pastorum,* lines 182–89. And compare the endings of the *Prima
Pastorum* and *Secunda Pastorum*—in one case "Syng we in syght"
(*PP,* 502), in the other, "To syng ar we bun: let take on loft" (*SP*
753–54)—with the ending of the *Judicium:*

> Therfor full boldly may we syng
> > On oure way as we trus;
> Make we all myrth and louyng
> > With te deum laudamus.
>
> > > > > > > (J., 617–20)

In the *Judicium* the two great themes which have informed the entire
Wakefield *Corpus Christi* play come to their finale. Evil men, satanic
figures in medieval terms, go to the "court" of their true prince, Satan,
closing the dramatic movement which began with Garcio in *Mactacio
Abel* and reached its peak in Pilate, in the tragic-phase plays and the
Resurreccio; and good men, men who by their nature partake in the
nature of Christ, typologically in the case of such Old Testament figures as Noah, Isaac, Jacob, and Moses, or symbolically in the case of
men like Symon, in the *Fflagellacio,* go to their reward in heaven.[6]

Doctrinally, of course, all this would be true of the history of mankind
—the *Corpus Christi*—whether or not it were carefully dramatized and
underscored by clever verbal devices. But in the Wakefield *Corpus
Christi* play it is dramatized, coherently and powerfully, making this
Corpus Christi play one of the most ambitious and impressive literary
works ever wrought by Englishmen.

The Wakefield Master:
Or, Does the Absence of a Camel
Imply the Absence of a Committee?

There is an old joke that a camel is a horse created by a committee. The pageants brought together in the Towneley MS have usually been considered a hodgepodge of literary texts, some very old, some fairly recent, some superb, some insipid, in which the sum of the parts is not really a whole but only a whole lot of parts. I have suggested in the foregoing chapters that this view is partly wrong, that in fact the Wakefield *Corpus Christi* play is not at all a literary camel but, despite lapses, a well-made work of art. I have tried to show that certain basic principles control the entire work. These principles may be summarized as follows:

First, many of the good men in the Old Testament who are traditionally viewed by church writers as types of Christ are insistently typologized, sometimes by the use of exegetical jokes of the kind I have pointed out in the Noah play and elsewhere, sometimes by other means. This sharpens the focus of the Old Testament plays on Christ, to whose Incarnation they look forward. The central technique involved in this typologizing of Old Testament figures—though not the sole technique—is realism-based allegory: Noah's wife, for instance, is a convincing real-life shrew (insofar as drama is ever "realistic") but her language and role illuminate Noah's allegorical role and her own, that is, respectively, Christ and the church.

Second, evil characters in both the Old and New Testaments are developed as satanic figures. To some extent this is a commonplace of the *Corpus Christi* cycles, but in the Wakefield cycle this treatment of evil figures is emphatic. The Wakefield writer's demonizing of Garcio in the *Mactacio Abel* may possibly involve reinterpretation of a minor character in the York pageant. (The York Brew-barret interpolation is from the mid-sixteenth century, but may reflect older tradition.) Garcio is, in any case, demonic, as Brew-barret is not. The Wakefield poet's substitution of Mak, in *Secunda Pastorum*, for the nondemonic religious burlesque in the *Prima Pastorum* points to this same concern with satanism (serious or comic) throughout the cycle. The feast in *Prima Pastorum* burlesques the feast of Christ (in addition to functioning in the way Professor Cawley pointed out), but it is, finally, just a physical feast. Mak, on the other hand, pretends to be the father he is not, bringing into the world the child (Lamb) he has not really fathered and ultimately suffering a blanket toss—a medieval means of bringing on labor. The Wakefield poet's contribution of an original Herod pageant—in which line after line of Herod's speech, or the speech of minor characters talking about Herod, burlesques biblical language about Christ and God the Father—shows the same thematic concern. And, finally, the poet's transformation of Pilate from the usual weak or dishonest man whose concern is, simply, peaceful government to the *mali actoris* of the tragic-phase pageants (that is, from the *Conspiracio* to the *Talentorum*), and the poet's elevation of Pilate to controlling villain in these pageants further indicate the poet's concern with focusing the drama as a conflict between Satan and Christ.

A third controlling principle is Professor Hardison's rule of fidelity to source. Certain kinds of speeches tend to remain stable, even in the most richly improvised pageants. Most notable among these are the speeches of Christ. Though the poet has added forty-two Wakefield stanzas to the *Judicium,* he does not improvise on the character of Christ. After the long dialogue of devils, he returns to his source for Christ's words (386 sq., et passim). As Professor Hardison has noted, the *Secunda Pastorum* is richly improvised down to the adoration scene, but that scene takes place quickly and simply, with no elaboration except for the tenderness introduced into the speeches of the shepherds.

What is involved in Professor Hardison's principle is not the poet's fear of saying something undoctrinal; neither is it simply a superstitious devotion to the actual language of the source, whether the source be the Bible, some popular lyric, or an older play. The poet's use of old materials is partly, and often primarily, aesthetic. Anyone who has read rhymed imitations of David's Psalms or the Canticle of Canticles knows how offensive such things can be. The same thing is involved when people object, as many did a few years ago, to new, more accurate translations of the Bible which displaced the "more poetic" King James. The same kind of vulgarization or at any rate unpleasant change is sometimes encountered in the realm of secular literature. Consider Walt Disney's *Pinocchio*. We may not always approve of the materials preserved in the patchwork plays, but we judge as aliens. The emotion which accrues to familiar lyrics rarely has much to do with their aesthetic value. On the other hand, the scissors and paste work is sometimes superb.

A fourth, more doubtful principle controlling revision may be the principle of dramatic rhythm. To rewrite the dull but serviceable Prophets' pageant (fragmentary in our text) would perhaps be to overextend the long line of anticipatory plays running from *Jacob* to *Salutacio Elezabeth*, in which (probably) only one, the *Pharao*, is allowed to develop into theatrical spectacle. Though most cycles must have included a Hanging of Judas pageant, the appearance of the *Suspencio Jude* at the end of the MS, out of place and written in a sixteenth-century hand, may be an indication that in this cycle it was in fact not performed or even included in the original collection, interfering, as it must, with the rounded action of the tragic-phase plays, *Conspiracio* through *Talentorum*, or the triumph group, *Extraccio* through *Judicium*. But obviously this is pure speculation. (The misplaced *Lazarus*, which belongs after the long John the Baptist pageant would perhaps be another strain on rhythm but was certainly designed for the cycle, including, as it does, several Wakefield stanzas.)

Of these four principles, I think only the fourth is thoroughly speculative. What the others appear to suggest is that someone, or some medieval playwriting committee, put together the entire Wakefield *Corpus Christi* play according to a plan. In its general outlines, it is the kind of plan we should expect from educated men who understood writing poetry according to the principles of exegetical grammarians. The first stage of composition—the stage of *inventio*—involved bringing together the diverse materials (the grammarians' assumption is that these will be largely traditional) which are to be used as major elements in the work. The second stage—*dispositio*—involved arranging the material, deciding what elements to highlight, what elements to play down, and so on. And the third involved fleshing the skeleton: amplifying some parts, shortening others, weaving the whole together by means of various kinds of rhythmic encoding (verbal repetition, the repetition of key images or emblems, and other devices). I have discussed elsewhere ways in which this theory of *translatio* effects the poetry of Chaucer, the *Gawain*-poet, the *Beowulf*-poet, Cynewulf.[1] In all of these poets' work it will be discovered that parts of the given finished poem *are brought over intact from the source.* Skeat's or Robinson's notes on Chaucer show that the *Book of the Duchess,* for instance, is a tour de force of quotation. Chambers's study of *Beowulf* shows that, even though we usually cannot tell where the poet found his materials, we can be sure that he borrowed heavily.[2] So did Cynewulf.[3] The *Gawain*-poet's quotation of old materials is limited only by the necessity of framing them in alliterative verse. The vision section of the *Pearl* is straight out of the *Apocalypse:* many passages in *Patience* and *Purity* are straight biblical translation; and in *Sir Gawain and the Green Knight* the poet leans heavily not only on Romance tradition (as Larry Benson has shown[4]), but also on his own earlier poems, ringing very slight changes on passages from *Purity.* I need hardly mention Malory's borrowing, or Langland's.

So far as poetic *method* is concerned, the chief difference between the Wakefield *Corpus Christi* play and all the Old and Middle English poems I have mentioned is one of size. Within the context of the *Corpus Christi* play's leviathan rhythm, the quotation of an entire older pageant is hardly more a proof of disjointedness or unoriginality than is a quotation by Chaucer of, say, six lines from Machault.

Then is the Wakefield *Corpus Christi* play the work of a committee of medieval playwrights working independently, or is it the work of a single poet-reviser or, at least, master designer?[5]

The argument for shaping of the whole play by a single man, or by one man in close supervision of a group of poet-revisers goes as follows:

1. *Thematic control and unity of action.* The alternation of Christological and satanic materials, interspersed with simple devotional materials where no such allegorical extension is possible or desirable, makes the whole cycle a conflict of Christ and Satan which rises to a dramatic climax in the tragic-phase pageants, focusing on the agon of Christ and his satanic opponent Pilate; the final pageants reverse the drama, presenting the triumph of good over evil, Christ over Satan.

2. *Relative coherence of technique.* If the pageants are sorted into two groups, those which are central to the conflict of Christ and Satan, either literally or allegorically, and those which merely comment on the conflict, showing man's need for Christ, the Old Testament prophets' expectation of Christ, and the emotions of those to whom Christ comes—in other words, the "simple devotional plays"—we find possible indications of one playwright's (or redactor's) hand at work in all of the dramatically central pageants. Sometimes the indications are very clear, as in the pageants entirely composed in the Wakefield stanza; sometimes they are less clear but still marked, as in the *Mac-*

tacio Abel and the tragic-phase pageants which contain a few Wakefield stanzas or close approximations along with pronounced verbal
repetitions (e.g., *Consp.*, 24–27; *F.*, 23–26; *Judic.*, 143–48); and at times
the indications are relatively faint, as in the largely borrowed characterization of Pharao and the treatment of Moses as (in Pharao's eyes)
a warlock. If we set these three classes of pageants in columns, placing
under column I the pageants entirely composed in Wakefield stanzas,
under column II the pageants which contain at least a few Wakefield
stanzas and also contain other distinct signs of Wakefield Master au-
thorship (exegetical jokes, realistic comedy, detailed characterization,
social satire, and typical Wakefield Master words or phrases) and if
we place under column III pageants which may or may not contain
the Wakefield stanza but do contain all of the following: 1) broken-line
speeches like those pointed out in my earlier discussion of the *Abraham* and *Pharao* plays, 2) doubtful or unprovable allegory like that
perhaps present in the *Jacob*, 3) realistic diction, and 4) thematic
appropriateness supported by evidence that stanzas have been altered,
the results are as follows:

I	II	III
Processus Noe	Mactacio Abel[6]	Abraham
Prima Pastorum	Conspiracio	Jacob
Secunda Pastorum	Fflagellacio	Pharao
Magnus Herodes	Processus Crucis	Oblacio Magorum
Coliphizacio	Talentorum	Extraccio Animarum
	Judicium	Resurreccio Domini
	Lazarus	Peregrini
		Ascencio Domini

If we add a fourth group, pageants which show no sign of revision by
the Wakefield Master, it is this:

IV

Creation
Isaac
Prophetarum
Cesar Augustus
Annunciacio
Salutacio Elezabeth
Fugacio Jos. & Marie
Purificacio Marie
Pagina Doctorum
Johannes Baptista
Thomas Indie
[Suspencio Jude]

The coherence of technique through the entire Wakefield *Corpus Christi* is high, if we accept as a part of that technique the reworking and quotation of old materials. The pageants in group I are completely written in the Wakefield stanza, but the pageants in group II, which contain some Wakefield stanzas and some other forms, are equally intense works, so that any doubt we may have as to whether or not these pageants were written by the Wakefield Master or under his direct supervision, on his rhetorical plan, arises solely from the question, Why did he not revise completely? In most cases the principle of fidelity to source gives a possible answer; in others haste, laziness, or dependence on mere spectacle may be involved. The third group of pageants, most of which contain no Wakefield stanzas, is more doubtful. The *Extraccio Animarum* and the Abraham seem least doubtful. As for the *Resurreccio,* surely it is significant that Pilate has been introduced at the beginning, the poet departing from his source, that Pilate's character fits the Wakefield cycle's unique treatment of Pilate, and that characterization of Cayphas and Annas has been altered from the source to suit their characterization in the *Coliphizacio.* The *Pharao* is still more doubtful; but departures from the York source give Pharao lines echoed by Herod and Pilate in the Wakefield cycle; characterization of Pharao and Moses suits the scheme of the Wakefield play as a whole; and broken-line dialogue seems a fair indication of the Wakefield Master's hand or influence.

One way of suggesting the degree to which technique is coherent throughout the cycle is to note the total number of lines involved in each of the above groups:

I	2,777 lines
II	3,678 lines
III	3,631 lines
IV	2,515 lines
	12,601

Pageants entirely by the Wakefield Master (group I) make up just under a fourth of the entire cycle (2,777 lines out of 12,601). If we put groups I and II together, pageants written or heavily revised by the Wakefield Master, the two totals add up to just over half of the entire cycle. The total line-count of pageants which show no sign of having been revised by the Wakefield Master is only 2,515, and among these only *Cesar Augustus* bears or might bear, in revised form, directly on the controlling Christ-Satan or true lord–false lord conflict.

3. *Language.* A. C. Cawley points out in the introduction to *The Wakefield Pageants in the Towneley Cycle* that there are "distinct verbal parallels of an unconventional kind which help to line [the pageants] together," and he lists a number of these from Pageants II, III, XII, XIII, XVI, XXI, and XXX—*Mactacio Abel, Processus Noe, Prima* and *Secunda Pastorum, Magnus Herodes, Coliphizacio,* and *Judicium.*[7]

In the light of these considerations—thematic control and unity of action, coherence of technique, and the evidence of language—it seems natural to believe that the Wakefield Master did put together the Wakefield play or at least work out its master plan. (The latter supposition would seem to be supported by the introduction of thirteen-line and other irregular stanzas built on York models into plays also containing Wakefield stanzas.)

The Wakefield cycle is apparently not a product of years of pageant evolution in the city of Wakefield, but substantially a new work. Up through the fourteenth century, Wakefield was a small town, a sheep-crossing too small to afford a great cycle of plays. In the fifteenth century, however, Wakefield boomed;[8] among other signs of prosperity there is Wakefield's costly improvement of its church, which involved adding a new tower and painted glass windows. Its citizens wanted, and now could afford, a cycle like the one the guilds had at York. The all-day-long *Corpus Christi* play was the backbone of the festival that brought in farmers and villagers from miles around. The Wakefield church must have supported the idea, and it may have been through church influence that Wakefield got copies of pageants used in other towns, the pageants later adapted and revised to fit the master plan—a design analogous to an abbot's design for a cathedral. Little by little, the playwriting group or the one great playwright began to revise and rewrite—a few plays the first year, a few more the second, and so on. (If the job had been done all at once, we would not have two shepherd plays, both popular enough for inclusion in the official text.) When the work was finished, when the grand design had been realized, the crafts' copies were perhaps called in (filled with cross-outs, erasures, and inserts, sometimes very long inserts, as in the *Judicium*), and a copyist was hired to make a clean copy of the whole work—perhaps a register, as Professor Cawley thinks,[9] or perhaps simply a complete polished manuscript. The latter view would explain why the names of all the performing crafts were not written on the pageants when the manuscript was first compiled (as they are in the register of York plays) and why in the case of the five pageants which have the names of

crafts written on them, the craft names are in a sixteenth-century hand
—added, in other words, perhaps as much as a century after the writing of the manuscript. If these deductions are sound, the Wakefield
Master and any associates he may have had must have created the
Wakefield *Corpus Christi* play at about the time of the manuscript
which has come down to us, that is, about 1450 by L. Wann's dating,
or 1460 by the dating of S. de Ricci and W. J. Wilson, and in any case
no later than 1485 if we accept E. K. Chambers's judgment on the
scribal hand.[10]

  The aesthetic superiority of the Wakefield cycle comes partly from
the lateness of its creation. The playwright or playwrights who put it
together could steal all the latest devices for the stage (whether or not
they actually did so), and all the latest dramatic ideas (York realism,
for instance); moreover, since the hypothetical master playwright had
a starting point in the crude material of the older plays, he could concentrate on larger structural concerns—the rhythm of the *Corpus
Christi* play as a whole and the organizing idea of the Lenten agon.
He could take all that earlier pageant writers had done, could turn to
his purpose a stanza form whose nearest equivalent is in courtly lyrics,
and then, in accord with principles we have seen at work throughout
this study, could bind the whole huge play together, setting at all
climactic points masterpieces of his own.

Notes
Index

Notes

Prologue: The Wakefield Pageants

1. The Wakefield Master's use of comedy for allegorical purposes—a subject explored in several chapters of this book—has been treated by several critics, among them Donald F. Peel, "The Allegory in *Secunda Pastorum*," *Northwest Missouri State College Studies* 24 (1960), 3–11; Howard H. Schless, "The Comic Element in the Wakefield Noah," in *Studies in Medieval Literature in Honor of Professor Albert Croll Baugh* (London, 1961), pp. 229–43; Bernard McCabe, "The Second Shepherds' Play," *Explicator* 24 (1965), 534–38; Margery M. Morgan, " 'High Fraud': Paradox and Double-Plot in the English Shepherds' Plays," *Speculum* 34 (1964), 676–89; Alan H. Nelson, " 'Sacred' and 'Secular' Currents in the Towneley Play of Noah," *Drama Survey* 3 (1964), 393–401; Eugene Zumwald, "Irony in the Towneley Shepherds' Plays," *Research Studies of the State College of Washington* 25 (1958), 37–53; William M. Manly, "Shepherds and Prophets: Religious Unity in the Towneley *Secunda Pastorum*," *PMLA* 78 (1963), 151–55; J. V. Crewe, "The Wakefield Play of the Crucifixion," *Theoria* 22 (1964), 20–28; Eugene B. Cantelupe and Richard Griffith, "The Gifts of the Shepherds in the Wakefield *Secunda Pastorum*: An Iconographical Interpretation," *Mediaeval Studies* (Toronto) 28 (1966), 328–35; Joanne S. Altieri, "The Ironic Structure of the Towneley *Fflagellacio*, *Drama Survey* 7 (1969), 104–12; Clifford Davidson, "An Interpretation of the Wakefield *Judicium*," *Annuale Mediaevale* 10 (1969), 104–19, and, most elaborately, Walter E. Meyers, *A Figure Given: Typology in the Wakefield Plays* (Pittsburgh, 1970); and John Dennis Hurrell, "The Figural Approach to Medieval Drama," *College English* 26 (1965), 598–604. See also Donald James Savage, "An Analysis of the Comic Element in the Chester, York, Coventry, and Towneley Mystery Cycles," *Dissertation Abstracts* 16 (1956), 1017–18 (Minn.). Until very recently, scholarly attention was riveted on just a few plays, especially the Towneley *Secunda Pastorum* and *Noah*. Arthur Brown pointed out nearly a decade ago, in "The Study of English Medieval Drama," printed in *Franciplegius: Medieval and Linguistic Studies in Honor of Francis Peabody Magoun, Jr.* (New York, 1965), pp. 265–73, that what was then needed (and to

a large extent still is) is detailed study of medieval drama as it appeared in single localities, the kind of study which provides sufficient evidence to justify deduction and interpretation. For steps in this direction see, for example, Hans-Jürgen Diller, "The Craftsmanship of the 'Wakefield Master,'" *Anglia* 83 (1965), 271–88; D. C. Baker and J. L. Murphy, "The Late Medieval Plays of MS. Digby 133: Scribes, Dates, and Early History," *Research Opportunities in Renaissance Drama* 10 (1967), 153–66; Kenneth M. Cameron and Stanley J. Kahrl, "Staging the N-Town Cycle," *Theatre Notes* 21 (1967), 122–38, 152–65; Stanley J. Kahrl, "Medieval Drama in Louth," *Research Opportunities in Renaissance Drama* 10 (1967), 129–33; Paul H. Strohm, Jr., "The Dramatic and Rhetorical Technique of the Chester Mystery Plays," *Dissertation Abstracts* 27 (1966), 1467A (Berkeley, California); Catherine E. Dunn, "The Literary Style of the Towneley Plays," *American Benedictine Review* 20 (1970), 481–504; and Jeffrey A. Helterman, "Symbolic Action in the Plays of the Wakefield Master," *Dissertation Abstracts International* 30 (1970), 3430A (Rochester). By the nature of the case one cannot always limit oneself to analysis of a single cycle; there is too much evidence of borrowing from cycle to cycle, so that often understanding of the given playwright's work requires comparison of that work with plays from elsewhere. Some examples of comparative analysis, in addition to those already cited, are Alexandra F. Johnston, "The Christ Figure in the Ministry Plays of the Four English Cycles," *Dissertation Abstracts* 28 (1967), 632A–33A (Toronto); and Sister Mary M. Walsh, "The Judgment Plays of the English Cycles," *American Benedictine Review* 20 (1969), 378–94.

For a fairly standard view of the Wakefield Master as exceptional, "the first comedy-writer 'in English tongue,'" see A. P. Rossiter, *English Drama From Early Times to the Elizabethans* (London, 1950), pp. 74–75. For a less favorable view of the Wakefield poet, see Eleanor Prosser, *Drama and Religion in the English Mystery Plays: A Re-evaluation* (Stanford, California, 1961), pp. 3–18.

2. See Hardin Craig, *English Religious Drama of the Middle Ages* (Oxford, 1955), pp. 8–9, 19–150. Craig's view of how plays came to be expanded (new guilds needing new plays) is probably sound, despite the error of his general evolutionary theory. For evidence, see for instance, D. S. Bland, "The Chester *Nativity*: One Play or Two?" *Notes and Queries* 10 (1963), 134–35. For a good, brief commentary on prejudices and presuppositions in this standard view involved in theories of the evolution of the cycles, see J. Swart, "The Insubstantial Pageant," *Neophilologus* 41 (1957), 127–41. See also Arthur Brown, "The Study of English Medieval Drama," cited above. The book which virtually demolishes the evolutionary theory of Craig, Chambers, Young, and the rest is O. B. Hardison, Jr.'s *Christian Rite and Christian Drama in the Middle Ages* (Baltimore, Md., 1965). See also John Stevens's review of Hardison in *Medium Aevum* 36 (1967), 289–92.

3. See *The Towneley Plays*, ed. George England and Alfred W. Pollard, EETS, ES 71 (London, 1897), pp. xi–xiv.

4. See, for ample evidence, Rosemay Woolf, "The Effect of Typology on the English Mediaeval Plays of Abraham and Isaac," *Speculum* 32 (1957), 805–25. Cf. *The Towneley Plays*, pp. xi–xiv and xxvi–xxx; *York Plays*, ed. Lucy Toulmin Smith (1885, reprint ed. New York, 1963), p. xlviii. Further evidence comes from articles like that of John E. Bernbeck, "Notes on the Towneley Cycle *Slaying of Abel*," *JEGP* 62 (1963), 317–22, which trace the method of the plays to religious treatises or to traditional typology. Considerable work has been done along this line of late. A good early general statement is John Dennis Hurrell's "The Figural Approach to

Medieval Drama," cited above. See also Marjorie D. Downing's dissertation, "The Influence of the Liturgy on the English Cycle Plays," *Dissertation Abstracts* 27 (1967), 3424A (Yale); Alexandra F. Johnston's dissertation, "The Christ Figure in the Ministry Plays of the Four English Cycles" (cited above); and Edith Z. Gold's "Comedy and Theology in the Medieval Mystery Plays," *Dissertation Abstracts* 28 (1968), 2207A–8A (Michigan). See also Hardison, V. A. Kolve, *The Play Called Corpus Christi* (Stanford, California, 1966); Arnold Williams, "Typology in the Cycle Plays: Some Criteria," *Speculum* 43 (1968), 667–84; or—especially—Walter E. Meyers, *A Figure Given*, cited above.

5. *The English and Scottish Popular Ballads*, ed. Francis James Child (New York, 1956), vol. 2, no. 81, pp. 242 ff. For Mr. Niles's version, hear his recording, *The Ballads of John Jacob Niles, Tradition Records*, 1960, (TLP—1046).

6. See Eugene Vinaver, "Form and Meaning in Medieval Romance," *Modern Humanities Research* (Leeds, England, 1966), p. 4.

7. For instance Rosemay Woolf, cited above.

8. See W. L. Hildburgh, "English Alabaster Carvings as Records of the Medieval Religious Drama," *Archeaologia* 93 (1949), and Lawrence J. Ross, "Art and the Study of Early English Drama," *Renaissance Drama*, no. 6 (1963), 35–46. Cf. *n*27, below. See also Merle Fifield, *The Castle in the Circle*, Ball State Monograph no. 6 (Muncie, Ind., 1967).

9. Hardin Craig, p. 2.

10. See especially B. Hunninger, *The Origin of the Theatre* (The Hague, 1955) and the introduction to *Medieval Mystery Plays, Morality Plays, and Interludes*, ed. Vincent F. Hopper and Gerald B. Lahey (Great Neck, N.Y., 1962), pp. 20–34.

11. John Speirs, *Medieval English Poetry: The Non-Chaucerian Tradition* (London, 1957), pp. 307–18. Cf. his less temperate earlier version of the theory in *Scrutiny* 18 (1951–52), 86–117 and 246–65. J. Swart answers Speirs's theory in "The Insubstantial Pageant," pp. 137–38. Professor Hardison has shown how old Speirs's general approach and bias are and points to their presence in Chambers, Pierson, and others, pp. 14 ff.

12. O. B. Hardison, preface, p. ix, and pp. 253–83.

13. Prosser, p. 5.

14. Quoted by Hopper and Lahey, *Medieval Mystery Plays, Morality Plays, and Interludes*, p. 22. Cf. E. K. Chambers, *The Mediaeval Stage* (Oxford, 1903), 2:110.

15. Craig, pp. 7–8.

16. Ibid.

17. Prosser, pp. 3–18, 79–80, et passim.

18. See Hardison, pp. 35–79 et passim.

19. See Prosser, p. 80, and cf. chapter two.

20. Cf. G. R. Owst, *Literature and Pulpit in Medieval England* (London, 1933), especially p. 478.

21. Lawrence J. Ross, p. 28.

22. Prosser, p. 5.

23. Swart, pp. 132–34. On staging in general, see also Cameron and Kahrl, "Staging the N-Town Cycle," cited above, and Natalie C. Schmitt, "Was There a Medieval Theatre in the Round? A Reexamination of the Evidence," *Theatre Notes* 23 (1970), 130–42.

24. See E. K. Chambers, 2:114.

25. See Chambers, pp. 156 ff. On what was possible in England, as garnered from

descriptions of the early masques, see Enid Welsford, *The Court Masque* (Cambridge, 2927). See also Glynne Wickham, *Early English Stages, 1300–1600* (New York, 1959), vol. 1, *1300–1576*.

26. The striking example is the illustrative material in the Cotton Nero A.x. (*Pearl*, etc.), where mural techniques are turned to ms. illustration. See Sir Israel Gollancz facsimile edition, EETS.

27. See Durer's scene from the buffeting of Christ, reproduced by K. Mantzius, *A History of Theatrical Art* (London, 1903), 2: facing p. 38. Also reproduced in C. M. Gayley, *Plays of our Forefathers* (London, 1908), facing p. 8. Cf. the Grünewald frontispiece in A. P. Rossiter, *English Drama*. For a summary of discussion of drama's influence on art, see Louis Reau, *Iconographie de l'art chrétien* (Paris, 1957), 1:262 ff. See also W. L. Hildburgh, "English Alabaster Carvings as Records of the Medieval Religious Drama" and Lawrence J. Ross, "Art and the Study of Early English Drama," both cited above. Cf. M. D. Anderson, *Drama and Imagery in English Medieval Churches* (Baltimore, Md., 1963).

28. See Swart's comments and speculations, "The Insubstantial Pageant," pp. 132–33. And see, on French stages, Grace Frank, *The Medieval French Drama* (Oxford, 1954), pp. 171–72.

29. I borrow this charming fragment of a costume list from a talk by Merle Fifield at the 1966 Bi-annual Medieval Conference, Kalamazoo, Michigan. Cf. Rossiter, pp. 64–65.

30. *A Preface to Chaucer: Studies in Medieval Perspectives* (Princeton, N.J., 1963). For further discussion of the aesthetic behind the Wakefield cycle, see Walter E. Meyers *A Figure Given*, especially pp. 7–20.

31. Woolf. On realism-based allegory in post-medieval drama, see for instance Ross, "Art and the Study of Early English Drama," cited above.

One: Decorum and Satanic Parody in the Wakefield *Creation*

1. See Chambers, *The Mediaeval Stage* (Oxford, 1903), 2:71.
2. Hardin Craig, *English Religious Drama of the Middle Ages* (Oxford, 1955), pp. 8–9, 19–150.
3. George England and Alfred W. Pollard, eds., *The Towneley Plays*, EETS, ES 71 (London, 1897), p. 5*n*1.

Two: Theme and Irony in the *Mactacio Abel*

1. Two outstanding exceptions are Clifford Davidson's "The Unity of the Wakefield *Mactacio Abel*," *Traditio* 23 (1967), 495–500, and John E. Bernbeck's "Notes on the Towneley Cycle *Slaying of Abel*," *JEGP* 62 (1963). Relating the play to its most apparent influence, Ambrose's treatise *De Cain et Abel*, Bernbeck shows that the *MA* is a careful religious work. A more general approach than Bernbeck's is that of Oliver F. Emerson, "Legends of Cain," *PMLA* 21 (1906), 831–929. For typical early praise of the realism see P. Hamelius, "The Character of Cain in the Towneley Plays," *Journal of Comparative Literature* 1 (1903), 324–44.

2. Eleanor Prosser, *Drama and Religion in the English Mystery Plays: A Reevaluation* (Stanford, Calif., 1961), p. 80.

3. See especially chapter seven.

4. For the metaphor of cosmic feudalism see, for instance, Hugh of St. Victor, *On the Sacraments of the Christian Faith,* trans. Roy J. Defarrari (Washington, D.C., 1951), pp. 3–4, 28–29. For the commonplace view of the devil as king, sinners as members of the devil's court, see the discussion of the seven deadly sins in the *Ancrene Rewle.*

5. F. L. Ganshof, *Feudalism,* trans. Philip Grierson (New York, 1961), especially pp. 28 ff., 34 ff., 69 ff. And consider the symbolic significance of the ceremonial kiss, pp. 79 ff.

6. See Bernbeck, p. 317.

7. In "Langland's Piers Plowman," *The Age of Chaucer,* ed. Boris Ford (Baltimore, Md., 1954), Mr. Derek Traversi describes Langland's transformation of Piers into Christ as "daring." Insofar as Piers is a literal English plowman the description is valid, but the identification of the plowman as assiduous Christian and type of Christ is traditional. The well-known medieval lyric beginning "The merthe of all this londe Maketh the good husbande" is explicated, almost point for point, in Gregory's *Pastoral Care,* trans. Henry Davis, S.J., in *Ancient Christian Writers,* (Westminster, Md., 1950), 19:134 ff.

8. According to W. O. Hassell, the symbolic smoke of Cain's sacrifice is found in visual art from a period much earlier than the plays. See his review of M. D. Anderson's *Drama and Imagery in English Medieval Churches,* in *Medium Aevum* 33 (1964), 241–42.

9. The characterization of Garcio has some things in common with the Vice figure in the Morality play and also with folk play characters. See P. Happé, "The Vice and the Folk Drama," *Folklore* 75 (1964), 161–93.

10. If, with some readers, we take "harnes" to mean not armor but merely any sort of apparel (harness), the reading still holds. The parable of the wedding guest in tattered clothes provides a basis for identification of clothes and good works—an idea spelled out, for instance, in *Purity,* the alliterative poem.

11. J. Swart, "The Insubstantial Pageant," *Neophilologus* 41 (1957), 134–36.

12. See Hugh of St. Victor, p. 102.

13. Ganshof, p. 26.

14. In holding this view, Cain is doubtless not unlike many a hard-pressed medieval farmer in the audience, particularly the manor laborer cruelly taxed by a lord he has never met or even seen. See Sidney Painter, *Mediaeval Society* (Ithaca, N.Y., 1951), pp. 43–62.

15. Prosser, p. 79.

16. Cain's use of this weapon was almost certainly traditional, but this makes the point no less valid. See Professor Cawley's note to 1. 324. in *The Wakefield Pageants in the Towneley Cycle* (Manchester, 1958).

17. See Cawley's notes to lines 324 and 408.

Three: Christology in the Noah

1. See Howard H. Schless, "The Comic Element in the Wakefield Noah," in *Studies in Medieval Literature in Honor of Professor Albert Croll Baugh* (London, 1961), and Alan H. Nelson, " 'Sacred' and 'Secular' Currents in the Towneley Play of Noah," *Drama Survey* 3 (1964), 393–401. My comments on the play are mere footnotes to these articles.

2. See, for example, Hugh of St. Victor, *On the Sacraments of the Christian Faith*, trans. Roy J. Deferrari (Washington, D.C., 1951), pp. 14–15.

3. *The English Writings of Richard Rolle, Hermit of Hampole*, ed. Hope Emily Allen (Oxford, 1931), p. 113.

4. *Complete Works of the Gawain-poet* (Chicago, 1965), pp. 65–66. See also D. W. Robertson, Jr., *A Preface to Chaucer* (Princeton, N.J., 1963), pp. 70 ff., for the discussion of the tropology of Eden.

5. *The City of God*, trans. Marcus Dods (New York, 1950), p. 516. For Augustine's full account of the Noah story see pp. 516–26.

6. The comparison of Eve and Mary is a standard theme in the commentaries and appears in *Eva-Ave* paradox poems. See A. C. Cawley's comments in *The Wakefield Pageants in the Towneley Cycle* (Manchester, 1958), p. 96.

7. Lines 507–88. See also *Pearl*, ed. E. V. Gordon (Oxford, 1963), lines 541–76. Cf. the comic allusion to the grace-works debate (central to the Parable of the Vineyard) in *Secunda Pastorum* (309–14).

8. Cf. *Purity*, lines 35 ff.

9. The idea that a wife owes submission to her husband's "headship," analogous to the submission of the Church to her Head, was of course standard. See Sister Emma Therese Healy, *Woman According to Saint Bonaventure* (New York, 1956), especially pp. 79–115.

Four: Idea and Emotion in the *Abraham*

1. George England and Alfred W. Pollard, eds., *The Towneley Plays*, EETS, ES 71 (London, 1897), p. xxix.

2. See Hardin Craig, *English Religious Drama of the Middle Ages* (Oxford, 1955), pp. 306–9. Craig apparently views the Chester play as a transitional piece in which the first and second halves have no particularly meaningful relationship to one another, both coming from an older, fuller work; it is "still a mere succession of biblical events with one of them outgrowing the rest" (p. 306). The "York-Towneley complex" (as Craig calls the two plays) derives from "a simple scriptural play." He adds that "The York version has been vigorously rewritten after the separation of the cycles. The Wakefield version, much simpler in style and contents, may retain parts of the original play" (p. 307). The Dublin play "has dignity and no small amount of spirit," according to Craig (p. 308). The best play is the Brome (p. 309). For a similar evaluation see Joseph Quincy Adams, *Chief Pre-Shakespearean Dramas* (Cambridge, Mass., 1924), p. 117n1. Adams cites also the judgment of Lucy Toulmin Smith. Oddly enough, even Professor J. Swart seems to adopt this standard view. See his "The Insubstantial Pageant," *Neophilologus* 41 (1957), 140.

3. Quotations of the Chester play are from *The Chester Plays*, ed. Hermann Deimling, EETS, ES 62 (London, 1892), pt. 1.

4. Quotation of the Hegge pageant is from *Ludus Coventriae, or The Plaie called Corpus Christi*, ed. K. S. Block, EETS, ES 120 (London, 1922).

5. The text used for the Brome play is that of Joseph Quincy Adams. The standard text, improved by Adams, is that in *The Non-Cycle Mystery Plays*, re-edited for EETS by O. Waterhouse, ES 104 (London, 1909).

6. Professor Hardison quotes Amalarius's comment that "All previous sacrifices prefigured Him . . ." *Christian Rite and Christian Drama in the Middle Ages* (Baltimore, 1965), p. 60. This can of course be shown in spectacle. In conformity

with Augustine's typic view of Isaac (*City of God*, 16:32), illustrations in the black-books, in a misericord from Worcester, and elsewhere, Isaac carries faggots in the shape of a cross. See Lawrence J. Ross, "Art and the Study of Early English Drama," *Renaissance Drama*, no. 6 (1963), 38.

7. Quoted from *York Plays*, ed. Lucy Toulmin Smith (1885; reprint ed., New York, 1963).

8. Craig, pp. 306 ff.

Five: "Insipid" Pageants

1. A. P. Rossiter, *English Drama from Early Times to the Elizabethans* (London, 1950), p. 66.

2. On the various strata, see George England and Alfred W. Pollard, eds., *The Towneley Plays*, EETS, ES 71 (London, 1897), pp. xxvii ff.

3. O. B. Hardison, Jr., *Christian Rite and Christian Drama in the Middle Ages* (Baltimore, 1965), p. 251.

4. J. P. Migne, *Patralogia Latina* (Paris, 1844–64), 105:1118 ff.

5. Hardison, p. 57.

6. On the meaning of dew consider, for instance, Origen's remark in the "Exhortation to Martyrdom" (trans. John J. O'Meara, in *Ancient Christian Writers* [Westminster, Md., 1950], 19:62): "And who will not admit that on Ananias and his companions descended the spiritual benediction that is granted to all the saints and is spoken of by Isaac when he says to Jacob, *God give thee the dew of heaven,* rather than the physical dew which quenched the flame of Nabuchodonosor?"

7. *The City of God*, trans. Marcus Dods (New York, 1950), p. 560.

8. On the mystical significance of Jacob, see Gregory the Great, "Pastoral Care," trans. Henry Davis, S.J., in *Ancient Christian Writers* (Westminster, Md., 1950), 11:57; St. Ambrose, "Principal Works," trans. Rev. H. DeRomestin, in *Nicene and Post-Nicene Fathers of the Christian Church*, 2nd series (Grand Rapids, Mich., 1955) 10:21 and 190; St. John Crysostom, "Homilies," trans. Sister Thomas Aquinas Goggin, in *The Fathers of the Church* (New York, 1960) 41:416; St. Basil, "Exegetic Homilies," trans. Sister Agnes Clare Way, in *The Fathers of the Church*, 46:157. The Jacob mystery is a favorite of commentators, also treated by Jerome, St. Paulinus of Nola, Augustine (in several places), Sulptius Severus, and others.

9. *City of God*, pp. 560–61.

10. Ibid., p. 561.

11. From *Ludus Coventriae, or The Plaie called Corpus Christi*, ed. K. S. Block, EETS, ES 120 (London, 1922), pp. 245 and 254.

12. E. K. Chambers, *The Mediaeval Stage* (Oxford, 1903), 2:133–36.

13. See Rossiter, pp. 64–65; Chambers, 2:141–42, et passim.

14. J. Swart, "The Insubstantial Pageant," *Neophilologus* 41 (1957), 133.

15. Chambers, p. 138.

16. England and Pollard, pp. xvi–xvii.

17. The York text is quoted from Lucy T. Smith, as cited above, and the Towneley, when two citations are given, comes from the Surtees edition as reprinted by Lucy T. Smith below the York text; texts are cited here first with the Smith numbering, then with A. Pollard's.

18. "A Plea for the Study of the Corpus Christi Plays as Drama," *Studies in Philology* 26 (1929), 417.

Six: Light Dawns on Clowns

1. See, in addition to the brief remarks in Millicent Cary's *The Wakefield Group in the Towneley Cycle* (Baltimore, Md., 1930), A. C. Cawley's two notes, "Iak Garcio of the *Prima Pastorum*," *Speculum* 28 (1953), 169–72, and "The 'Grotesque' Feast in the *Prima Pastorum*," *Speculum* 30 (1955), 213–17; Catherine E. Dunn, "The Prophetic Principle in the Towneley *Prima Pastorum*," in *Linguistic and Literary Studies in Honor of Helmut A. Hatzfeld*, ed. Alessandro S. Crisafulli (Washington, 1964), pp. 117–27; H. A. Eaton, "A Source for the Towneley *Prima Pastorum*," *Modern Language Notes* 14 (1899), 265–68; Eugene E. Zumwalt, "Irony in the Towneley Shepherds' Plays," *Research Studies of the State College of Washington* 26 (1958), 37–53.

2. I've pointed out this same parodic method in the *Noe*, chapter three; see also chapters seven, eight, and nine.

3. On the coming of light as an advent theme, see B. G. Koonce, *Chaucer and the Tradition of Fame: Symbolism in the House of Fame* (Princeton, N.J., 1966), passim.

4. Cf. the serious focus on the washing of garments in *Pearl*, stanza 64, and the comic focus on the same in *Patience*, lines 341–42.

5. For the interpretation assumed here, see John Gardner, "Style as Meaning in the *Book of the Duchess*," *Language and Style* 2 (1969), 143–71.

6. A. C. Cawley, *The Wakefield Pageants in the Towneley Cycle* (Manchester, 1958), p. 113 (note to *Sec. Past.*, 718).

Seven: Structure and Tone in the *Secunda Pastorum*

1. On *Secunda Pastorum*, see (in addition to studies cited in the notes below): R. C. Cosbey, "The Mak Story and its Folklore Analogues," *Speculum* 20 (1945), 310–17; S. B. Hemingway, "English Nativity Plays," *Yale Studies in English* 38 (1909), 28; Bernard McCabe, "The Second Shepherds' Play," *Explicator* 24 (1965), 534–38; F. J. Thompson, "Unity in the *Second Shepherds' Play*," *Modern Language Notes* 64 (1949), 302–6; Eugene E. Zumwalt, "Irony in the Towneley Shepherds' Plays," *Research Studies of the State College of Washington* 25 (1958), 37–53.

2. For discussion of the medieval idea that women are to be ruled by their husbands as Christ's Mystical Body, the church, is ruled by Christ and as the state is ruled by the king, see Sister E. T. Healy, *Woman According to Saint Bonaventure* (New York, 1956), particularly the section entitled "Women in Nature." I have argued elsewhere that this idea is central to the medieval vision. The same symbolic relationship of marriage, Christianity, and feudalism informs Chaucer's "Marriage Group" (see John Gardner, "The Case Against the 'Bradshaw Shift'; or, the Mystery of the Manuscript in the Trunk," *Papers on Language and Literature* 3 supplement [1967], 80–106 and especially 92–104) and also informs *Sir Gawain and the Green Knight*.

3. I do not take account in this discussion of William M. Manly's view of the shepherds as prophets, Mak as false prophet. ("Shepherds and Prophets: Religious Unity in the Towneley *Secunda Pastorum*," *PMLA* 78 [1963], 151–55.) Professor Manly's reading and my own are complementary.

4. *Religious Lyrics of the XIVth Century*, ed. Carleton Brown (Oxford, 1924), lyric no. 28.

5. Giving the sheep a "turne" need not mean driving them away to spite Coll and Gyb. See Professor Cawley's note to lines 136 sq. *The Wakefield Pageants in the Towneley Cycle* (Manchester, 1958), p. 106. Sheep grazing on a "balk" must not be allowed to wander into fields devoted to crops; hence the sheep must occasionally be turned. "Ye ar two all-wyghtys" is doubtless simply the grumbling—not necessarily heart-felt—of the servant who feels that his masters (or his master and his master's friend) are slave-drivers. It is true that the poet plays the word "all-wyghtys" (monsters) against the earlier talk of "meruels," but it is not necessary to assume bitterness in Daw to account for the humor in the sudden juxtaposition. The lines which follow next,

> Bot full yll haue I ment;
> As I walk on this bent,
> I may lyghtly repent
> My toes if I spurne

mean simply (as E. Talbot Donaldson glosses them) that turning the sheep is a bad idea because, walking in the dark, one might stub one's toes.

6. The song has been identified as a descant in three parts. Considering the importance of the number three throughout the play, one might imagine the shepherds' final song (at the end of the play) as another three-part descant; but perhaps three voices in unison would serve the symbolic purpose. (On the song as descant, see H. Traver, "The Relation of Musical Terms in the Woodkirk Shepherds' Plays to the Dates of their Composition," *Modern Language Notes* 20 (1905), 1–5).

7. J. H. Smith, "Another Allusion to Costume in the Work of the 'Wakefield Master,' " *PMLA* 52 (1937), 901–2.

8. The parable and all its elaborate implications are worked out in *Pearl*, a poem the Wakefield Master may have known. Some of the Master's phrases faintly echo phrases in the *Pearl*-poet's treatment of the parable, for instance *swange and swat* (*Pearl*, 586) and *the long day* (*Pearl*, 597); and the central concern of both poets is order and the perversion of order, for the *Pearl*-poet the "courtesy" of vassal and lord in the Christian scheme. But both the ideas and the phrasing are conventional.

9. Professor Cawley points out that, loosely speaking, the pattern throughout is *Coll-Gyb-Daw*. A more precise breakdown may be of interest: From line 115 (just before Daw's entrance) to the end of the first movement, the speeches alternate regularly in the pattern *Coll-Gyb-Daw* with only two interruptions (at lines 261–64 and 370–74); in the second movement the speeches alternate, after the opening stanza (449–57), in the unbroken pattern *Daw-Coll-Gyb;* in the third movement, after the opening stanza (629–37), the speeches alternate in the unbroken pattern *Coll-Gyb-Daw*, as in the first movement. It is possible to explain the regularity of alternation throughout the play in a practical fashion by arguing that it simplified the work of the actors. But such regularity is to be found nowhere else in the mystery plays. Another possible explanation, supported by our observations concerning the structural balance of the play, is that the Wakefield Master quite simply enjoyed working out patterns. Perhaps a third explanation is also possible. The regular alternation of speeches may conceivably reflect an equally stylized stage focus: it would be appropriate that the serious and reflective Coll be given stage-center in the first and third movements, and that the child, Daw, be given stage-center for the second, farcical movement.

10. The idea evidently behind this system of characterization—an idea not much developed in this play or in *Prima Pastorum* where it also appears, as we have seen —is the medieval commonplace of the tripartite soul. In Scholastic thought man has three souls in one: the rational soul (reason), the concupiscent soul (loosely, the desiring faculty), and the irascible soul (loosely, spirit or mettle). Man's spiritual welfare depends on right reason, right desire, right assiduity, qualities which win man salvation. Perverse reason (cunning or habitual reflection upon lower things), perverse desire (carnal as opposed to spiritual desire), and perverse irascibility (wrath as opposed to assiduity, loyalty, or righteous indignation) lead to man's damnation. Since the time of the fall, even the healthy function of the tripartite soul cannot in itself save man; but the healthy soul is open to grace, that is, to supplemental force for the rational, concupiscent, and irascible souls through, respectively, God's wisdom, God's love, and God's power—the attributes of Father, Son, and Holy Ghost (or by another account, Son, Father, Holy Ghost). See Hugh of St. Victor, *The Didascalicon,* trans. Jerome Taylor (New York, 1961), bk. I, or see Hugh's *On the Sacraments of the Christian Faith,* trans. Roy J. Defarrari (Washington, D.C., 1951), pp. 31 ff., et passim. The shepherds in the *Secunda Pastorum* are only vaguely related to the healthy activities of the tripartite soul—Coll as the rational, Gyb as the concupiscent, Daw as the irascible—but Mak and Gill are directly related by their actions to the three perversions of soul. It is significant that Mak and Gill are *two*—the number of discord, duality, or the devil.

11. For more detailed treatment of these traditional symbols, see Lawrence J. Ross, "Art and the Study of Early English Drama," *Renaissance Drama,* no. 6 (1963), 39 and *n*13, 45; and Eugene B. Cantelupe and Richard Griffith, "The Gifts of the Shepherds in the Wakefield *Secunda Pastorum:* An Iconographical Interpretation," *Medieval Studies* 28 (1966), 328–35.

Eight: Christian Black Comedy

1. George England and Alfred W. Pollard, *The Towneley Plays,* EETS, ES 71 (London, 1897), p. xxvii.

2. Cf. for instance, *Pearl,* stanza 94.

3. *Pearl,* stanza 51.

4. A. C. Cawley, *The Wakefield Pageants in the Towneley Cycle* (Manchester, 1958), p. 117, note to line 325.

Nine: The Tragicomedy of Devil Worship

1. On the movements in the cycle, see J. Swart, "The Insubstantial Pageant," *Neophilologus* 41 (1957), 139; Jerome Taylor, "The Dramatic Structure of the Middle English Corpus Christi, or Cycle, Plays," in *Literature and Society: Nineteen Essays by Germaine Bree and Others* (Lincoln, Neb., 1964); and O. B. Hardison, Jr., *Christian Rite and Christian Drama in the Middle Ages* (Baltimore, Md., 1965), pp. 253–83. The idea that the whole of a cycle is meant to be seen as one vast play is becoming a commonplace. See Catherine E. Dunn, "The Medieval 'Cycle' as History Play: An Approach to the Wakefield Plays," *Studies in the Renaissance,* 7 (1960), 76–89 (the unified history of God's plan for mankind).

2. Swart's theory of double acting convention is more applicable to these plays

than in *Magnus Herodes,* perhaps, where the women at first seem to joke with the soldiers. In the five-play sequence at hand, the evil torturers are certainly bustling, squealing, impish creatures, and Pilate a roaring tyrant, both contrasting with the solemnly acted Christ, Mary, John, and so on. See Swart, pp. 134–36. Cf. J. W. Robinson, "Medieval English Acting," *Theatre Notes* 13 (1959), 83–88, and "Three Notes on the Medieval Theatre," *Theatre Notes* 16 (1962), 60–62.

3. Hardison, pp. 81–82. Gustaf Aulén's book is *Christus Victor: An Historical Study of the Three Main Types of the Idea of Atonement,* trans. A. G. Herbert (New York, 1951); see especially chap. 8, pp. 4–7, 16–60.

4. On Pilate in the Towneley MS, see Arnold Williams, "The Characterization of Pilate in the Towneley Plays," *Michigan State College Studies in Language and Literature* (East Lansing, Mich., 1950), pp. 72–73, and Sister Nicholas Maltman, O.P., "Pilate as *Malle actoris*," *Speculum* 36 (1961), 308–11.

5. The identification of Satan as "God of the ground" is commonplace. See, for instance, the frequent use of this phrase in the Belshazzar section of *Purity.*

6. See T. McAlindon, "Comedy and Terror in Middle English Literature: The Diabolical Game," *Modern Language Review* 60 (1965), 323–32. Also on demonic comedy see William G. McCollom, "From Dissonance to Harmony: the Evaluation of Early English Comedy," *Theater Annual* 21 (1964), 69–96. E. K. Chambers, with his anticlerical bias, regularly viewed devils and devil figures as evidence of the recrudescence of pagan instinct and so viewed the comedy as a sort of implied criticism of the Christian doctrine carried by the plays. (See, for instance, *The Mediaeval Stage* [Oxford, 1903], 2:147–48.) Karl Young gives a more modern view, saying that they were "undoubtedly . . . an object of derision as well as of fear, but in a particular dramatic situation we may not be able to say confidently which effect was intended or achieved" (*The Drama of the Medieval Church* [Oxford, 1933], 2:406–7). Again, see Professor Hardison's first essay in *Christian Rite and Christian Drama.*

7. A. C. Cawley, *The Wakefield Pageants in the Towneley Cycle* (Manchester, 1958), p. 122, note to line 358.

8. See Charles Thomas Samuels, "The Dramatic Rhythm of the Wakefield Crucifixion," *College English* 22 (1961), 343–44.

Ten: The Comic Triumph

1. O. B. Hardison, Jr. treats the reversal as the Resurrection alone (*Christian Rite and Christian Drama in the Middle Ages* [Baltimore, Md., 1965], p. 287). My disagreement is trifling, really a matter of strategy, since my concern is to show how at Wakefield the whole play is brought together in the last movement.

2. Ibid.

3. See George England and Alfred W. Pollard, eds., *The Towneley Plays,* EETS, ES 71 (London, 1897), pp. xviii–xix.

4. See Arnold Williams, "The Characterization of Pilate in the Towneley Plays," *Michigan State College Studies in Language and Literature* (East Lansing, Mich., 1950), pp. 72–73, and Sister Nicholas Maltman, O.P., "Pilate as *Malle actoris*," *Speculum* 36 (1961).

5. This is a convenient place to note that I do dismiss without a word the *Lazarus* and *Suspencio Iude,* the latter probably not a part of the original cycle.

6. For interesting further comment on the *Judicium,* see Hazel Dean McClure,

"Eschatological Theme in English Medieval Drama," *Emporia State Research Studies* 14 (1965), 14–28, especially 23–25.

Epilogue: The Wakefield Master

1. Chaucer in, for instance, my "Style as Meaning in the *Book of the Duchess*," *Language and Style* 2 (1969), 143–71; the *Gawain*-poet in *The Complete Works of the Gawain-Poet* (Chicago, 1965), especially pp. 55–84; the *Beowulf*-poet in "Fulgentius' *Expositio Virgiliana Continentia* and the plan of *Beowulf*," *Papers on Language and Literature* 6 (1970), 227–62; Cynewulf in "Cynewulf's *Elene*: Sources and Structure," *Neophilologus* 54 (1970), 65–76.

2. R. W. Chambers, *Beowulf: An Introduction to the Study of the Poem*, 3rd ed., rev. by C. L. Wrenn (London, 1967), e.g., pp. 48–111, et passim.

3. See Claes Schaar, *Critical Studies in the Cynewulf Group* (Copenhagen, 1949), for observations on Cynewulf's use of diverse sources in signed poems.

4. *Art and Tradition in Sir Gawain and the Green Knight* (New Brunswick, N.J., 1965).

5. Arnold Williams, in "The Characterization of Pilate in the Towneley Plays," *Michigan State College Studies in Language and Literature* (East Lansing, 1950), presents a convincing argument that the tragic-phase pageants are the work of one playwright.

6. Professor Martin Stevens points out to me that this play contains only one true Wakefield stanza, #35, and that this one is not arranged in the nine-line formation in the MS.

7. A. C. Cawley, *The Wakefield Pageants in the Towneley Cycle* (Manchester, 1958), pp. xviii–xix.

8. For the history of Wakefield, see E. J. Walker, *Wakefield, Its History and People*, 3rd ed. in 2 vols. (Wakefield, Yorkshire: S. R. Publishers, Ltd., 1964). Originally printed by the West Yorkshire Printing Co., Ltd., Wakefield, 1939.

9. Cawley, p. xii. For detailed discussion, see Martin Stevens, "The Accuracy of the Towneley Scribe," *The Huntington Library Quarterly* 22 (1958), 1–9.

10. Cawley, p. xin2.

Index

Garcio *(cont.)*
 ing the audience, 38; compared to Pi-
  late, 109, 122; as persecuted slave, 112;
  compared to Morality play vice figure,
  147n9
Garcio, Jack, 78, 81
Gawain-poet, 27, 135, 136, 154n*1*
Gifts: in *Secunda Pastorum*, 95
Gill: relationship with Mak, 89, 90; com-
  pared to Eve, 90; compared to the
  Virgin, 90
God: in York Cycle, 17; relationship of
  Cherubim to, 20; in conflict with Sa-
  tan, 22; Cain's debt to, 33; in the
  Wakefield Noah, 41, 42, 48; in the
  Wakefield *Abraham*, 63; ball as a sym-
  bol of, 95
Gollancz, Sir Israel, 146n26
Gospel, the, 45, 69
Gower, John, 27
Gregory, 28
Guilds, 2, 5, 9, 65, 70, 139
Gyb: as a clown, 78, 79; as symbol of
  concupiscent soul, 79, 80; representing
  charitable love in *Secunda Pastorum*,
  86, 92, 93, 94, 95, 129; mentioned,
  151n5, 151n9, 152n*10*

Hamlet, 4
Hardison, O. B., 4, 5, 9, 66, 67, 105, 106,
  120, 134, 145n*12*, 149n*3*, 149n5, 153n*1*,
  153n2
Harmony vs. discord: main theme of the
  Wakefield Noah, 40, 41, 42, 57; in the
  Abraham, 52
Harrowing of Hell, discussion of, 29, 65,
  71, 74, 105, 120
Heaven, Christ's ascension to, 70
Hegge Cycle, 2, 13, 16, 49, 52–53
Hell, smoke and stench as emblems of,
  28
Herod: dramatically parodic of God, 18,
  22, 97; as a Satanic figure, 22, 103;
  compared to Cesar, 71, 73, 75; comedy
  in speeches of, 75; in the *Oblacio
  Magorum*, 96; in *Magnus Herodes*,
  98–102; discussion of, 105, 118, 122,
  134, 138
Holy Ghost, bird as symbol of, 95

Horn, Jack: as a fierce clown, 78; as
  irascible soul in *Prima Pastorum*, 79,
  80
Icarus, Lucifer compared to, 19
Iliad, the, 10
Incarnation: in the *Abraham*, 52; in
  Prima Pastorum, 79
Isaac: part of the typology of the Wakefield cycle, 7, 10; in the Brome *Abraham*, 55; in the York *Abraham*, 56; in
  the Wakefield *Abraham* typology, 57;
  in the Wakefield *Abraham*, 61–64, 67,
  68; mentioned, 131
Isaac pageant: reference to missing frag-
  ments of, 64; not characteristic of
  Wakefield poet's work, 65; spectacle in,
  67 allegory in, 67, comedy in, 67;
  Christ typology in, 67, 68; dramatic
  techniques used in, 68; verbal realism
  of, 68
Ishmael, son of Abraham, 56

Jacob: typic of Christ, 68, 71; men-
  tioned, 67, 131
Jacob pageant: as relates to the *Isaac*,
  65, 68; dramatic techniques in, 68, 69;
  verbal realism in, 68, 69; Christ typology in, 69; as good spectacle, 70,
  71; mentioned, 135, 137, 149n*8*
Jews, 72
John, the Disciple (or Beloved), 115,
  153n2
John the Baptist, 104, 105, 135
Jonah, 26
Jonson, Ben, 8
Joseph of Arminthea, 116
Judas, as a stock villain, 110
Judicium: improvisation in, 9; sources
  of, 129; jokes on singing in, 131;
  themes of, 131; discussion of, 134–35,
  139

Kamptowne, 99
"King of Kings," 22
Kittredge, G. L.: on "The Marriage
  Group," 26

Lactanius, 83
Langland: concept of Do-Best, 27; use of
  allegory by, 27; mentioned, 136

Summer Sunday, in reference to the *Oblacio Magorum,* 96

Suspencio Jude, 135, 153n5

Symeon, 104

Symon of Cyrene: discussion of, 115–16; as symbolic of Christ, 131

Talentorum, the: discussion of, 104, 116, 122, 134–35; as part of tragic-phase pageants, 134–35

Thomas Indie, 128, 129

Tithe: of Cain and Abel, 30; worthless 35; in the Wakefield *Abraham,* 50

Towneley Manuscript: missing parts of, 19; discussion of, 71

Tragic-phase pageants, 134–35, 137

Trial of Christ: reference to Wakefield version of, 65

Trinity: as central to the Wakefield Noah pageant, 40, 42; thematic center of *Secunda Pastorum,* 40, 92, 95; in *Prima Pastorum,* 78, 81; mentioned, 108

Troilus, 26

Troilus and Criseyde: love vs. power in, 26

Turkey: in *Magnus Herodes,* 99

Tuskane: in *Magnus Herodes,* 99

"Twa Sisters, The," 14

Typology, in mystery plays, 12. *See also* Christ; God; Satan

Ubi sunt form, 61. *See also Abraham,* the

Uxor: typic of Eve or the Virgin, 43; comic and thematic source, 42–47, 80; mystical body, 45; typology of repentance, 46; mentioned, 97, 133

Vanitas, vanitatum tradition, 87. *See also Secunda Pastorum*

Vanity Fair, 78

Verbal devices: repetition (echo), 20, 51, 54, 58, 80, 132, 137, 138; realism in the *Jacob,* 68–69. *See also* Realism

Vergil, in *Prima Pastorum,* 83

Vice figure: in Morality plays, 147n9

Vinaver, Eugene, 3

Virgin: Uxor typic of, 43; emblem of charity in *Secunda Pastorum,* 86–87;

speech in *Secunda Pastorum,* 91; mentioned, 26

Vulgate Cycle, 4

Wakefield Cycle: missing parts of, 14; evolution of, 15–16

Wakefield Master: characteristics of, 2, 15; compared to York Poet, 16; in reference to the *Creation,* 21–22; in reference to the *Mactacio Abel,* 23; as a revisionist, 69, 74; in reference to *Magnus Herodes,* 103; as a social satirist, 130; as author of Wakefield cycle, 134–40

Wakefield Noah pageant: light imagery in, 40, 41, 47, 48; feudalism in, 42; compared to the other Noah pageants, 42; main themes of, 42, 47, 61; comedy in, 43, 47, 73, 76; fall of the proud in, 48; compared to the *Abraham,* 61; compared to the *Oblacio Magorum,* 97; mentioned, 119, 139. *See also* Noah.

Wann, L., 140

Williams, Arnold, 154n5

Wilson, W. J., 140

Witchcraft, in the pageants, 123

Woman's advice: danger of, 90; stock idea in *Secunda Pastorum,* 90

Woolf, Rosemary, 12, 146n31

York *Abraham* pageant: compared to the Wakefield *Abraham,* 49, 61, 62; discussion of, 56–58; contrasted with the Brome *Abraham,* 57; blindfold motif in, 57

York *Creation* pageant: structural parallels of, 19–20

York Cycle: discussion of, 2, 13, 119, 120, 124–25, 138; compared to the *Magnus Herodes,* 102; realism in, 140

York XI (eleven). *See Departure of the Israelites from Egypt*

York *Massacre of Innocents:* role of Mahowne in, 98

York Metrist. *See* York Poet

York Poet: discussion of, 15; compared to the Wakefield poet, 16; concern with reality in drama, 20